Discover Financial Freedom Even with Variable Income

Flexible Strategies to Handle Fluctuations, Grow Wealth, and Gain Lasting Confidence

By: Alex Bradley

© Copyright Silver Valley Publishing 2024 – All rights reserved.

The content within this book may not be reproduced, duplicated or transmitted without direct written permission from the author or the publisher.

Under no circumstances will any blame or legal responsibility be held against the publisher, or author, for any damages, reparation, or monetary loss due to the information contained within this book. Either directly or indirectly. You are responsible for your own choices, actions, and results.

Legal Notice:

This book is copyright protected. This book is only for personal use. You cannot amend, distribute, sell, use, quote or paraphrase any part, of the content within this book, without the consent of the author or publisher.

Disclaimer Notice:

Please note the information contained within this document is for educational and entertainment purposes only. All effort has been expended to present accurate, up-to-date, and reliable, complete information. No warranties of any kind are declared or implied. Readers acknowledge that the author is not engaging in the rendering of legal, financial, medical or professional advice. The content within this book has been derived from various sources. Please consult a licensed professional before attempting any techniques outlined in this book.

By reading this document, the reader agrees that under no circumstances is the author responsible for any losses, direct or indirect, which are incurred as a result of the use of the information contained within this document, including, but not limited to, — errors, omissions, or inaccuracies.

"Do not save what is left after spending, but spend what is left after saving."

-Warren Buffett

Contents

Introduction 9

Chapter 1: Understanding Irregular Income and Financial Basics 11

   1.1 Embracing the Unpredictability of Income 11

   1.2 Financial Literacy: Breaking Down the Basics 12

   1.3 The Psychology of Money: Shifting Your Financial Mindset 14

   1.4 Common Pitfalls of Irregular Income Management 16

   1.5 Emotional Resilience Across Income Types 18

   1.6 Legal and Tax Considerations for Diverse Income Types 20

   1.7 Income Variability: Transforming Challenges into Opportunities 22

   1.8 Building a Resilient Financial Foundation 24

Chapter 2: Creating a Flexible Budgeting System 26

   2.1 Using Technology: Budgeting Apps That Work 28

   2.2 Seasonality Trends in Different Industries 32

   2.3 Leveraging Predictive Models and Tools 34

   2.4 Budgeting with a Purpose: Allocating Every Dollar 36

   2.5 The Art of Adjusting: Flexibility in Budgeting 37

   2.6 Navigating Cash Flow: Strategies for Smoothing Income 40

   2.7 Overcoming Objections: Making Budgets Work for You 41

Chapter 3: Debt Management and Reduction Techniques 44

   3.1 The Debt Avalanche vs. Debt Snowball: Choosing Your Path 46

   3.2 Evaluating Profitability 48

   3.3 Breaking Free: Psychological Wins in Debt Reduction .. 50

   3.4 Innovative Debt Management Tools and Resources 52

3.5 Avoiding Debt Traps: Strategies for Long-Term Success 53

3.6 Rebuilding Credit: Steps to Improve Your Financial Health 54

Chapter 4: Building and Maintaining an Emergency Fund...... 57

4.1 Small Steps, Big Impact: Starting Your Savings Journey 60

4.2 Finding Hidden Savings: Unearthing Opportunities 61

4.3 Reflection Section: Uncover Your Savings 63

4.4 Protecting Your Fund: Strategies to Avoid Dipping In ... 64

4.5 Creative Ways to Boost Your Emergency Savings........... 66

Chapter 5: Strategic Savings and Investment Planning 69

5.1 Introduction to Investment: Where to Begin 71

5.2 Diversifying Income Streams: Building Passive Income 75

5.3 Retirement Planning for Irregular Earners..................... 79

5.4 Future-Proofing Finances: Embracing Emerging Trends 81

Make a Difference with Your Review 84

Chapter 6: Enhancing Financial Literacy and Mindset 87

6.1 Financial Education: Resources for Continuous Learning 88

6.2 Mindset Shifts for Financial Empowerment 90

6.3 Overcoming Financial Anxiety with Knowledge 92

6.4 The Role of Emotions in Financial Decisions 98

6.5 Building a Community of Financial Support 102

Chapter 7: Adapting to Life Changes and Transitions............ 103

7.1 Financial Planning for Major Life Events 103

7.2 Transitioning to Self-Employment: Financial Considerations... 105

7.3 Navigating Marriage, Divorce, and Family Dynamics .. 109

7.4 Balancing Finances in Single-Income Households 111

7.5 Preparing for Parenthood: Financial Readiness............ 113

7.6 Embracing Change: Financial Resilience Amidst Transitions.. 116

Chapter 8 Achieving Long-Term Financial Goals................... 118

8.1 Avoiding Lifestyle Inflation: Staying on Track 121

8.2 Tracking Progress and Celebrating Milestones: Staying Motivated on Your Financial Journey 123

8.3 Leveraging Income Flexibility for Financial Growth 126

8.4 Trusts and Estate Planning Tools for Legacy Building . 127

8.5 Building a Legacy: Long-Term Wealth and Security..... 130

Conclusion.. 133

References 136

About the Author... 142

Introduction

There's a familiar feeling for many of us who face irregular incomes. It's a sense of uncertainty when the end of the month approaches, and the numbers just don't add up. You might be a freelancer, a bartender, a farmer, or a real estate agent. Some months, you're riding high with more than enough. Other times, you're wondering how to stretch a dime until the next payday. This book is for you and anyone else who knows the stress and frustration of an unpredictable paycheck.

I'm Alex Bradley, and I understand those challenges firsthand. Growing up on a farm, I saw my family work tirelessly, only to face financial instability time and again. We had to manage with what we had, often stretching resources to their limits. These experiences shaped my understanding of money and motivated me to find solutions. Today, I'm a seasoned entrepreneur and financial strategist. I've spent years navigating the complexities of variable income streams, not just for myself but for countless others who share this journey.

The purpose of this book is simple: to empower you to achieve financial stability, build wealth, and gain confidence in your financial decisions, even with a variable income. It's about transforming uncertainty into a manageable asset, allowing you to thrive no matter what your paycheck looks like each month.

Many people face issues such as financial instability, difficulty budgeting, and the stress of unpredictable cash flow. According to one survey, nearly 60% of individuals with irregular incomes report feeling anxious about their financial future. (FINRA, 2021) When you don't know how much you'll earn, traditional budgeting advice just doesn't cut it. You need strategies tailored to your unique situation.

Here's what you can expect from this book: practical strategies and solutions that you can apply immediately. We will cover budgeting techniques, saving methods, and investment tips that cater to fluctuating incomes. You'll learn how to turn financial unpredictability into an asset, using your income's flexibility to your advantage. This isn't just another personal finance book. It's a guide specifically for you—the variable income earner. What sets this book apart are the real-world examples and actionable advice that speak directly to your experiences and needs.

This journey begins with understanding the nature of irregular income—both the challenges it presents and the opportunities it creates. First, we will lay the foundation for building a financial plan that works for your unique circumstances. Let's start by exploring the core principles of managing variable income and setting the stage for financial confidence and freedom.

Chapter 1: Understanding Irregular Income and Financial Basics

Life with an irregular income can feel like riding a roller coaster without a safety harness. Each month brings its own set of surprises, and financial planning can seem like an elusive dream. For many of you, this is an all-too-familiar reality. Whether you're a farmer whose income depends on the harvest, a freelancer juggling multiple projects, or a bartender pocketing tips, the unpredictability of income isn't just a side note—it's your everyday existence. You're not alone in this, and understanding the nature of your income is the first step toward gaining control and peace of mind.

1.1 Embracing the Unpredictability of Income

Irregular income takes many forms, each with its own rhythm and demands. Freelancers and gig economy workers often face fluctuating earnings dictated by client contracts and seasonal demands. One month, you might find yourself flush with cash, juggling multiple projects and deadlines. The next, you're scouring job boards, hoping for the next gig to materialize. It's a lifestyle that offers freedom but demands relentless hustle. Commission-based roles, like those in real estate or sales, add another layer of complexity. Success can bring significant rewards, but dry spells may leave you counting pennies. Meanwhile, farmers and other seasonal workers face the ebb and flow of nature and market demands. Their livelihoods hinge on factors beyond their control, such as weather conditions and crop yields, which makes financial predictability a constant challenge. Even those with side hustles or part-time jobs experience this unpredictability, as their supplementary income sources fluctuate with varying demand and availability.

While irregular income can be unpredictable, it also offers unique benefits. Flexibility is one of its greatest assets, allowing you to carve out a lifestyle that suits your rhythm. You can work when you want and prioritize the projects or tasks that matter most to you. This freedom can lead to a fulfilling work-life balance where you're not tied to a nine-to-five schedule. However, this flexibility comes with its challenges. Financial stress can loom large when income isn't guaranteed, making budgeting and planning complex. The inconsistency can be daunting, often leading to anxiety about meeting financial obligations. But here's the opportunity: by embracing this irregularity, you can develop a mindset of resilience and adaptability. Viewing income variability as an opportunity rather than a hindrance opens doors to creative financial strategies and solutions.

1.2 Financial Literacy: Breaking Down the Basics

Financial literacy is the cornerstone of making informed financial decisions, especially when dealing with variable income. To truly grasp the nuances of personal finance, we must familiarize ourselves with key terms and concepts.

Two pivotal terms in this domain are cash flow and net worth. Cash flow refers to the movement of money in and out of your accounts, which is crucial for understanding your financial health. It's the pulse of your finances, indicating whether you're living within your means or overspending. Net worth, on the other hand, is the snapshot of your financial standing. It's calculated by subtracting liabilities from assets. This figure gives a clear picture of your wealth at any given moment. Understanding concepts like budgeting and savings is vital. Budgeting involves creating a plan for your money, allowing you to allocate funds for necessities, savings, and discretionary spending. Savings, meanwhile, act as a buffer for unexpected expenses and future goals. A lack of knowledge in these areas can lead to poor financial decisions. Many have found themselves in debt because they misunderstood cash flow or failed to budget effectively. For instance, not recognizing the difference between gross and net income can lead to overspending, as the money available for discretionary spending is often less than initially perceived.

Empowering yourself with financial literacy enables you to make decisions that align with your financial goals. To support this, numerous resources are available. Books like "The Total Money Makeover" by Dave Ramsey or "Rich Dad Poor Dad" by Robert Kiyosaki offer foundational knowledge. Online courses from platforms like Coursera or Khan Academy provide structured learning opportunities. These resources teach you how to navigate the complexities of personal finance. They enhance your ability to create a personal budget, a vital tool for those with irregular incomes. Budgeting allows you to prioritize spending, ensuring that essentials are covered while allocating funds for savings and debt repayment. Understanding credit scores is another practical application of financial literacy.

Your credit score influences your ability to secure loans, rent apartments, and even get certain jobs. By knowing what affects your score, you can take steps to improve it, such as paying bills on time and reducing debt.

The journey to financial literacy is ongoing. It requires a commitment to learning and applying new knowledge. Engaging with these resources and concepts will help you build a robust financial foundation. As you become more literate, you'll find that making sound financial decisions becomes second nature. The confidence gained from understanding your finances empowers you to face any challenges that arise. This knowledge is not just theoretical; it has real-world implications, affecting every aspect of your financial life. By investing time in education, you equip yourself with the tools needed to navigate the financial landscape effectively.

1.3 The Psychology of Money: Shifting Your Financial Mindset

Money is not just about numbers; it's deeply intertwined with our thoughts, emotions, and beliefs. Our relationship with money often begins in childhood, shaped by the financial attitudes we observe and absorb from those around us. Whether you grew up in a household where money was plentiful or scarce, these early experiences can influence how you view and manage your finances today. Common fears and insecurities about money might arise from these roots—worrying about never having enough, fearing debt, or feeling overwhelmed by financial decisions. It's crucial to recognize how these ingrained beliefs can impact your financial behavior. For instance, someone who grew up in a financially insecure environment might develop a scarcity mindset, leading to anxiety-driven spending or hoarding money without investing in growth opportunities.

Embracing a growth mindset can be transformative in personal finance. A growth-oriented approach encourages you to see challenges as opportunities to learn and improve. This mindset shift allows you to view financial setbacks not as failures but as stepping stones toward better financial health. The benefits of adopting this perspective are manifold; it cultivates resilience, fosters optimism, and enhances problem-solving skills. With a growth mindset, you're more likely to set realistic financial goals, adapt to changing circumstances, and ultimately achieve greater financial satisfaction. By focusing on what you can learn from each experience, you empower yourself to take proactive steps toward financial well-being.

Shifting your financial habits begins with identifying and overcoming limiting beliefs. Start by reflecting on your current attitudes toward money: Do you see it as a tool for empowerment or a source of stress? Recognize any negative patterns that might hold you back, such as impulse spending or avoidance of budgeting. Setting and achieving financial goals is another crucial step in transforming your financial mindset. Begin with small, attainable targets to build momentum and confidence. Your mindset will naturally shift toward greater financial discipline and optimism as you accomplish these. Incorporating strategies like creating a vision board with your goals or journaling about your financial aspirations can help reinforce these changes.

Incorporating psychological tools can further enhance your financial mindset. Mindfulness practices, such as meditation or deep-breathing exercises, can reduce stress and improve focus, allowing you to make more intentional financial decisions. Financial affirmations, positive statements about money and abundance, can rewire your thinking, replacing fear and doubt with confidence and clarity. For instance, repeating affirmations like "I am capable of managing my finances" or "I am open to new financial opportunities" can gradually transform your financial mindset. These practices, combined with a commitment to personal growth, can help you build a robust financial foundation, even amidst the uncertainties of irregular income.

1.4 Common Pitfalls of Irregular Income Management

Managing irregular income is fraught with potential pitfalls, and many of these arise from common financial mistakes that people make without even realizing it. One frequent error is **overspending during high-income months**. It's a natural inclination to indulge when the paychecks are larger, leading to a lifestyle that feels celebratory but is ultimately unsustainable. For instance, a bartender might find themselves with a surplus after a bustling holiday season, only to splurge on a new gadget or vacation. This kind of spending offers short-term satisfaction but can create long-term financial distress. When the income dips, as it inevitably will, those splurges can transform into burdens, leaving one scrambling to meet basic expenses. This cycle of feast and famine is compounded by neglecting to save for lean periods, a mistake that many fall into. *The temptation to forego savings in favor of immediate gratification can be overwhelming, but it leaves individuals vulnerable when income slows.* It's not just a matter of lacking funds; it's about the stress and anxiety that accompany the inability to cover unexpected expenses. The consequences of these mistakes are profound. Accumulating debt is a major risk, with credit cards often serving as a temporary solution that spirals into a long-term problem. The inability to handle unexpected expenses—whether it's a car repair or a medical bill—only adds to the instability, further eroding any sense of financial control.

To counter these pitfalls, several strategies can be employed to maintain a balanced financial life. **Establishing a buffer or emergency fund** is one of the most effective measures. This fund acts as a financial safety net, providing support during times of low income. Ideally, it should cover three to six months of essential expenses, offering peace of mind and reducing reliance on credit.

Regular financial reviews are another crucial strategy. By routinely assessing your financial situation, you gain a clear picture of your income and outgoings, allowing for timely adjustments. **Automated savings apps** can be invaluable tools in this regard. They simplify the process of saving by automatically setting aside a portion of your income, ensuring that you're consistently building a safety net without needing to think about it. Financial experts often emphasize the importance of such proactive measures. They advocate for budgeting techniques that align with your income's ebb and flow. For instance, adopting a rolling budget that adjusts each month based on actual income can provide greater flexibility and control. Additionally, they suggest maintaining a separate account for savings, which can help prevent impulsive spending and safeguard your financial future.

All of these elements center on living within your means and planning for variability. I can't stress enough the importance of developing a budget that caters to both high and low-income months, ensuring that you're never caught off guard. By prioritizing savings and maintaining a disciplined approach to spending, you can navigate the challenges of irregular income with confidence and stability.

1.5 Emotional Resilience Across Income Types

For many, the emotional toll of living with a fluctuating income can be as daunting as the financial aspects themselves. Take, for instance, the bartender who relies heavily on tips. In bustling months, the money flows freely, but during quieter times, the anxiety of insufficient earnings can be overwhelming. This volatility breeds stress, making it challenging to maintain a steady financial footing. Farmers face a different set of pressures, their income tied to the seasons and the whims of nature. One bad crop and the financial plans they laid can unravel, leaving them to ponder the next steps over the long winter months. Freelancers, too, live in a world of uncertainty, juggling client commitments and the constant search for new work. The stress of not knowing when the next paycheck will come can cast a long shadow over their personal and professional lives.

Managing these stressors requires more than just financial acumen; it necessitates **emotional resilience**. Developing resilience means building the capacity to adapt to change and bounce back from setbacks. One effective technique is **stress management**, which can take many forms.

We hear the term stress management thrown around so often that we forget that it is an actual management process that we can employ to our benefit at any time. **Mindfulness and meditation practices** can help calm the mind, offering a moment of peace amidst the chaos. Regular exercise and proper nutrition are crucial in maintaining mental health, providing the energy and clarity needed to tackle financial challenges head-on.

Likewise, joining **peer support communities** can offer a lifeline. These in-person or online groups provide a space to share experiences, offer advice, and lend an empathetic ear. For example, freelancers often find solace in online forums where they can discuss everything from client management to financial planning, drawing strength from shared experiences. Platforms like Meetup.com are excellent for finding local or virtual groups tailored to specific interests, such as personal finance, freelancing, or small business management. Social media platforms, particularly Facebook and LinkedIn, host countless groups focused on financial education and community support. Searching for hashtags like #MoneyTips or #FreelancerSupport can uncover resources tailored to your needs.

For those seeking more structured environments, nonprofit organizations such as SCORE offer free workshops and mentoring for small business owners. Many local libraries or community centers also host financial literacy events or regular support group meetings. By actively engaging with these communities, you can gain practical insights, build accountability, and foster a sense of belonging as you navigate the challenges of managing irregular income.

Developing a network of peers who understand the unique challenges of variable income can open doors to new opportunities and solutions. Engaging with others in similar situations provides a sense of camaraderie and reduces the isolation that often accompanies financial strain. These communities can also provide practical advice, offering insights into how others have successfully managed their stress and maintained their financial stability. Through these connections, individuals can learn about new tools, resources, and strategies they might not have discovered.

Emotional resilience isn't built overnight, but it can be nurtured and developed through consistent effort and support. By prioritizing mental well-being and seeking out supportive networks, those navigating the challenges of variable income can foster a stronger, more adaptable mindset. This resilience not only aids in weathering the financial storms but also enhances overall quality of life, providing a foundation for sustainable financial success.

1.6 Legal and Tax Considerations for Diverse Income Types

Navigating the intricacies of legal and tax obligations can be daunting for those with variable incomes, yet it's crucial to maintaining financial health. Self-employed individuals, including freelancers, gig workers, and entrepreneurs, face a distinct set of tax responsibilities compared to traditional employees. Unlike standard W-2 employees, those with irregular incomes must grapple with self-employment taxes covering Social Security and Medicare. These are akin to the payroll taxes that employers typically withhold. However, the onus is on self-employed individuals to calculate and pay these taxes themselves. This involves a more comprehensive approach to record-keeping. Keeping meticulous records of income and expenses is vital, as tax deductions—such as those for office supplies, travel, and professional development—can significantly reduce taxable income. For instance, a freelance writer might deduct the cost of a laptop, while a real estate agent could claim travel expenses incurred while showing properties. This level of detail requires diligent tracking, often facilitated by spreadsheets or accounting software that categorizes expenses for easy retrieval during tax season.

A common pitfall for many in this demographic is underestimating the **quarterly estimated tax payments** required by the IRS. Unlike salaried employees, whose taxes are withheld automatically, self-employed individuals must project their annual income and remit taxes in quarterly installments. Failure to do so can lead to penalties and a hefty tax bill come April. The IRS provides tools such as Form 1040-ES to help calculate these payments, yet many neglect this step, leading to financial strain. Another frequent mistake is not setting aside a portion of each paycheck for taxes, leaving individuals scrambling for funds when payments are due. This oversight can be mitigated by adopting a disciplined approach, such as *automatically transferring a percentage of each payment* into a separate tax account, ensuring funds are available when needed.

Several tools and strategies can aid in managing these responsibilities. Accounting software like QuickBooks or FreshBooks streamlines the tracking of income and expenses, making it easier to compile the necessary information for tax filings. These platforms often integrate with banking systems, providing real-time updates and reducing the likelihood of errors. Additionally, **hiring a tax professional can offer peace of mind**. They can navigate the complexities of tax law, optimize deductions, and ensure compliance with all regulations. For those new to self-employment, this investment can pay dividends in the form of saved time and reduced stress. Many financial institutions offer credit cards that contribute to retirement accounts, like a Roth IRA, providing a dual benefit of managing expenses while planning for the future.

Understanding and adhering to legal and tax obligations not only ensures compliance but also fosters financial stability. By proactively managing these aspects, individuals with variable incomes can avoid common pitfalls, optimize their financial strategies, and focus on growth and prosperity. The key lies in adopting a proactive approach, leveraging available tools, and seeking professional guidance when necessary.

1.7 Income Variability: Transforming Challenges into Opportunities

Income variability often feels like a storm brewing on the horizon, unpredictable and relentless. Yet, within this uncertainty lies a hidden potential for growth and opportunity. When viewed through a different lens, **variable income can become a catalyst for financial development**. One way to harness this potential is by diversifying income streams. By not relying solely on a single source, you can create a buffer against the volatility of any one income channel. Consider someone who starts as a freelance writer but later expands to offer online writing workshops. This diversification not only provides additional revenue but also taps into new markets and opportunities. The same principle applies to a real estate agent who invests in rental properties, creating passive income that complements their commission-based earnings.

Another avenue for transforming income variability into an asset is investing in skill development. As the job market evolves, equipping yourself with new skills increases your adaptability and marketability. This continuous learning can open doors to higher-paying gigs or entirely new career paths. Picture a graphic designer who takes courses in digital marketing. This added expertise allows them to offer a broader range of services, attracting a wider clientele and commanding higher fees. By investing in yourself, you create a dynamic career path that adjusts to the changing tides of income.

There are countless examples of individuals who have successfully navigated the challenges of variable income. Take Zach, an entrepreneur who launched a small online business during a period of financial uncertainty. Initially, it was a side project, a way to supplement their main income. But they transformed it into a thriving enterprise through strategic planning and leveraging digital tools. Or consider a side hustler named Sara who started selling handmade crafts on an online marketplace. With dedication and smart marketing, they grew their hobby into a profitable venture, illustrating how income variability can fuel entrepreneurial spirit and innovation.

To manage income variability effectively, several tools and techniques can be employed. Budgeting apps and software provide a structured way to track and plan finances, allowing for adjustments as income fluctuates. Apps like Mint or You Need a Budget (YNAB) can offer insights into spending patterns and help in setting realistic financial goals. Automated savings plans are another practical tool. By automatically diverting a portion of income into savings, you create a financial cushion without conscious effort. This automated discipline helps in building security over time, mitigating the effects of unexpected income changes.

Proactive financial planning is crucial in harnessing the potential of variable income. Setting clear financial milestones can guide your path, providing a roadmap for financial success. Regularly monitoring monthly cash flow allows for timely adjustments and ensures that you remain on track to meet your goals. With these strategies, you can transform the challenges of income variability into opportunities for growth and financial empowerment. As you achieve these milestones, you'll feel a sense of pride and accomplishment in your financial journey.

1.8 Building a Resilient Financial Foundation

Remember that we are setting ourselves up for *lifetime stability, not just short-term survival.* Establishing this resilient financial foundation means creating a stable, robust base that can withstand the ebbs and flows of irregular income. It's about laying down a framework that supports your financial well-being despite the unpredictability of earnings. The key components of such resilience include emergency savings, diversified income streams, and prudent spending habits. These elements ensure that when income dips or unexpected expenses arise, you have the safety nets in place to absorb the shocks without derailing your financial plans. This sense of security will provide you with peace of mind and reassurance in the face of income variability.

Building this resilience requires actionable steps and commitment. Start with establishing a realistic savings plan. Begin by **setting aside a small percentage of your income each month**, gradually increasing as your financial situation improves. This steady, disciplined approach will help you accumulate savings over time. **Reducing unnecessary expenses** is another critical step. Examine your spending habits, **identifying areas where you can cut back** without compromising your quality of life. Redirecting these savings into your emergency fund or investments can create a more secure financial future.

Creating a resilient financial foundation is an ongoing process that requires dedication and adaptability. It involves making informed choices, setting realistic goals, and being prepared for the unexpected. By implementing these strategies, you can build a financial safety net that supports your goals and aspirations, allowing you to navigate the challenges of irregular income with confidence.

As you progress, remember that financial resilience is not just about having money; it's about ensuring that you can maintain your lifestyle and achieve your goals, no matter what life throws your way.

Chapter 2: Creating a Flexible Budgeting System

Picture yourself standing in front of a blank canvas, paintbrush in hand, ready to create a masterpiece from the unpredictable colors life offers. That's how budgeting with a variable income feels. It's an art form requiring creativity, adaptability, and a keen sense of balance. The colors you choose—your income streams and expenses—must work together, forming a cohesive picture of financial stability. For many, managing an irregular income feels like trying to paint in the dark. But with the right tools and techniques, you can illuminate the path to financial clarity, transforming chaos into a masterpiece of financial security. In this chapter, we explore zero-based budgeting, a method designed to bring structure and order to the unpredictable nature of variable income.

Zero-based budgeting is a concept that turns traditional budgeting on its head. Instead of starting with the previous month's expenses and making slight adjustments, this approach begins each month with a clean slate. The idea is simple yet powerful: allocate every dollar of your income before the month begins, ensuring that your income minus your expenditures equals zero by month's end (NerdWallet, n.d.). This system encourages you to scrutinize each expense, promoting mindful spending and ensuring that your financial goals, such as savings and debt repayment, are met. Using the previous month's income to plan for the current month can mitigate some of the unpredictability inherent in variable income, allowing for more consistent financial management (Gobler, n.d.).

Creating a zero-based budget involves several key steps. First, **list all sources of income** and their expected amounts. This might include your primary job, side hustles, freelance work, or any other income streams. Next, **categorize your expenses** into fixed, variable, and savings categories. Fixed expenses are those that remain constant each month, such as rent or mortgage payments. Variable expenses fluctuate and might include utilities, groceries, or transportation costs. **Savings** should be treated as a non-negotiable expense, contributing to your financial security and future goals. Once you've listed your income and expenses, **allocate funds accordingly**, ensuring that every dollar has a purpose. This meticulous approach provides a clear snapshot of your financial health, allowing for adjustments as income fluctuates.

For those with variable incomes, zero-based budgeting offers distinct advantages. It provides enhanced control and clarity over your finances, making it easier to track spending habits and identify areas for improvement. This system encourages you to adjust your budget with each new income cycle, fostering adaptability and resilience. For a freelance graphic designer, this might mean allocating more funds to marketing during slower months to attract new clients. Meanwhile, a gig economy driver might prioritize maintenance and fuel costs during busy periods, ensuring their vehicle is always ready for work. By embracing the principles of zero-based budgeting, you gain a comprehensive understanding of your financial landscape, empowering you to make informed decisions.

Crafting Your Zero-Based Budget

1. **List Your Income Sources**: Write down all sources of income you expect for the upcoming month. Include everything from your main job to side gigs.

2. **Categorize Expenses**: Divide your expenses into fixed, variable, and savings. Include essentials like rent and groceries under fixed expenses.

3. **Allocate Funds**: Assign every dollar to a category until your income equals your expenses. Adjust as necessary to ensure balance.

4. **Review and Adjust**: At the end of each month, review your budget. Identify areas for adjustment and plan for the next month.

Through these steps, you create a financial framework that offers stability and clarity, even amidst the fluctuations of a variable income.

2.1 Using Technology: Budgeting Apps That Work

The advantages of using technology in budgeting are manifold. Apps simplify the often daunting task of financial management, providing real-time data that's crucial for making timely decisions. Automation plays a significant role here, as apps can track expenses automatically, categorize them, and alert you when you're nearing budget limits. This means less time spent manually entering data and more time focusing on other important areas of your life. Budgeting apps offer the convenience of having your entire financial picture at your fingertips. You can access this data from anywhere, whether you're at home, at work, or on the go. Alerts for overspending or approaching limits ensure you stay on track, helping to prevent financial mishaps.

Budgeting Apps: Finding the Right Fit

Budgeting apps simplify tracking income and expenses, making it easier to implement a flexible system that adapts to the ups and downs of irregular cash flow. Two standout options, **YNAB (You Need a Budget)** and **Mint**, cater to different budgeting styles and preferences, offering unique benefits to users.

- **YNAB (You Need a Budget):** This app's zero-based budgeting framework helps users allocate every dollar they earn to a specific purpose, ensuring that no money is left unaccounted for. It is particularly effective for those with irregular incomes, as it allows you to prioritize spending and savings based on your unique financial situation. YNAB's tools for goal tracking and reporting provide valuable insights into your progress, helping you stay motivated. While YNAB requires a hands-on approach, its detailed system can transform the way you manage money, giving you full control over your finances.

- **Mint:** For those who prefer automation, Mint offers a more passive approach to budgeting. It syncs directly with your bank accounts and credit cards to track spending and income in real time. Mint's automated categorization of expenses and visual insights into spending patterns make it a great choice for individuals seeking simplicity. While it may lack the intentionality of YNAB's approach, Mint is ideal for those who want to monitor their finances with minimal effort.

When it comes to choosing the right app, personal preferences and needs should guide your decision. Look for a user interface that is intuitive and easy to navigate. If an app feels cumbersome or confusing, you're less likely to use it consistently. Another critical factor is the integration with your banking systems. Apps that can seamlessly connect with your bank accounts, credit cards, and investment portfolios provide a more accurate financial overview. Consider what features are most important to you, whether it's expense tracking, bill reminders, or goal setting. Some apps offer free versions with basic functionalities, while others may require a subscription for advanced features.

Feedback from users who have successfully managed their finances with these apps can offer valuable insights. For example, Sarah, a freelance graphic designer, used YNAB to regain control over her unpredictable income. The app's structured framework allowed her to allocate funds during peak months and build a cushion for slower periods. On the other hand, Mint's automation helped James, a part-time consultant, gain clarity on his spending patterns without requiring daily manual updates. These testimonials highlight the practical benefits of embracing digital tools for budgeting. By leveraging technology, you can transform how you manage money, gaining control and confidence in your financial journey.

The Role of Accountability Partners and Financial Coaches

Consistency is key to successful budgeting and external support can make a world of difference. Accountability partners and financial coaches provide the encouragement and guidance needed to maintain focus and achieve financial goals.

Accountability Partners

An accountability partner could be a trusted friend, family member, or colleague who understands your financial goals and checks in regularly on your progress. These partners act as a sounding board for your financial decisions, helping you stay motivated and disciplined. For instance, scheduling monthly reviews with an accountability partner can provide a shared sense of responsibility and make budgeting a collaborative effort.

Financial Coaches

For a more structured approach, financial coaches offer professional support tailored to your needs. Unlike financial advisors, who focus on investments and long-term strategies, financial coaches concentrate on day-to-day money management and behavior change. They help you develop realistic budgets, set achievable goals, and navigate complex financial decisions. Platforms like **The Financial Gym** connect individuals with certified financial coaches, offering personalized strategies and regular check-ins.

James, a self-employed photographer, found success by partnering with a financial coach. Together, they developed a budget that accommodated his irregular income and set savings targets for peak months. The coach's expertise and accountability helped James build a six-month emergency fund within a year, giving him peace of mind and financial stability.

Putting It All Together

Combining the use of budgeting apps with the support of accountability partners or financial coaches can significantly enhance your ability to manage an irregular income. Whether you're taking a hands-on approach with YNAB, automating your tracking with Mint, or seeking external guidance, these tools and relationships provide the structure and motivation needed to succeed. With the right support system in place, you can navigate financial uncertainty with confidence and clarity.

2.2 Seasonality Trends in Different Industries

Seasonality plays a significant role in shaping the financial landscape for many industries. For those working in fields like farming, real estate, or hospitality, understanding and anticipating these trends is crucial for maintaining financial stability. Farmers, for instance, live by the rhythm of the seasons, where income hinges on the success of the harvest. A bountiful season translates into financial security, while a poor yield can spell economic hardship. This cyclical nature requires farmers to manage their cash flow carefully, often setting aside reserves during peak times to tide them over during off-seasons. Similarly, real estate professionals experience market booms and lulls. The spring and summer months often bring a flurry of activity, with buyers eager to move before the school year starts. However, as winter approaches, the market can slow, leading to leaner months. Those in hospitality face similar ebbs and flows. A hotelier in a tourist town might see bustling business during holiday seasons, only to face a lull in the off-season. Understanding these patterns helps in planning ahead, ensuring that the high tides cover the low.

To manage cash flow effectively during these high and low seasons, strategic planning is key. One effective strategy is to build a cash reserve during peak income months. This reserve acts as a financial buffer, allowing you to cover fixed expenses during slower periods without dipping into emergency funds. We will explore emergency funds in greater detail later on, but to get started lets look at a couple of examples. A farmer might save extra from a profitable harvest to cover equipment maintenance in the winter. Similarly, a real estate agent could allocate a portion of their commissions during busy months to cover marketing expenses during quieter times.

Building Your Emergency Fund

1. **Assess Your Needs**: Calculate three to six months' worth of living expenses, considering housing, utilities, groceries, and transportation.
2. **Set a Savings Goal**: Determine the total amount you need for your emergency fund based on your assessment.
3. **Create a Savings Plan**: Decide on a weekly or monthly savings target that fits your budget, even if it's a small amount.
4. **Track Your Progress**: Use an app or spreadsheet to monitor your savings growth and adjust your plan as needed.

Another approach is to diversify revenue streams. Farmers might explore selling value-added products like jams or pickles, providing year-round income. Real estate professionals could offer consulting services or host workshops on home buying, tapping into new markets and income sources. In hospitality, offering off-season packages or hosting events can keep cash flowing when tourist numbers dwindle.

Proper cash flow management also involves forecasting and budgeting based on historical data. By analyzing past seasons, you can predict income patterns and plan accordingly. This foresight allows for proactive adjustments, such as scaling back on non-essential expenses during low-income months. It also helps in identifying opportunities to invest in growth during peak seasons. For example, a hotel might renovate or upgrade facilities when cash flow is strong, enhancing long-term profitability. In farming, investing in sustainable practices or diversifying crops during profitable years can yield future benefits. By integrating these strategies, individuals and businesses can maintain financial stability despite the inherent unpredictability of seasonal trends.

2.3 Leveraging Predictive Models and Tools

In today's digital age, using technology to forecast earnings offers a strategic advantage for individuals with variable incomes. *Predictive models and tools powered by artificial intelligence and historical data can provide insights that are invaluable for financial planning.* These tools analyze past income patterns, market trends, and even economic indicators to project potential earnings. QuickBooks, for example, is a favorite among freelancers for its ability to track income and expenses, generate financial reports, and forecast cash flow based on historical data. This not only helps in understanding current financial health but also in anticipating future changes, allowing you to make informed decisions about budgeting and saving.

For those in agriculture, tools like AgPlan cater specifically to the unique needs of farmers. They offer financial planning and analysis features that help manage cash flow throughout the year, considering seasonal variabilities and crop cycles. By leveraging such tools, farmers can better predict income fluctuations, prepare for lean seasons, and make strategic investments during peak times. This foresight is crucial in industries where external factors like weather and market demand largely dictate income. With accurate predictions, financial planning becomes less of a guessing game and more of a calculated strategy.

The integration of these predictive tools into your financial routine can streamline the budgeting process, offering a clearer picture of future financial scenarios. They provide real-time updates and alerts, enabling you to adjust your financial plans in response to changing circumstances. This adaptability is particularly beneficial for entrepreneurs and side hustlers, who often juggle multiple income streams. By using predictive models, you can identify patterns and trends that might not be immediately apparent, opening up opportunities to optimize income and reduce financial stress.

Choosing the right predictive tool involves assessing your specific needs and preferences. Consider the complexity of your income streams, your comfort level with technology, and the type of insights you require. Some tools offer comprehensive features, including tax calculations and investment analysis, while others focus on basic income and expense tracking. The key is to find a tool that aligns with your financial goals and provides the level of detail you need to make informed decisions. Many of these tools offer free trials, allowing you to explore their features before committing, ensuring they fit seamlessly into your financial management strategy.

Incorporating predictive models into your financial planning empowers you to take a proactive approach to managing your finances. By anticipating changes and preparing accordingly, you can mitigate risks and capitalize on opportunities, ensuring stability even in the face of income variability. This strategic use of technology not only enhances your ability to manage day-to-day finances but also lays the groundwork for long-term financial success. With the right tools, you can navigate the complexities of variable income with confidence, turning potential challenges into opportunities for growth and prosperity.

2.4 Budgeting with a Purpose: Allocating Every Dollar

Budgeting is more than just numbers on a spreadsheet; it's about aligning your spending with what truly matters to you.

Intentional spending means taking control by prioritizing needs over wants and making sure that your money reflects your values. It's about making choices that resonate with your life goals rather than being swayed by fleeting desires. For instance, consider the difference between buying a new gadget because everyone else has it and saving for a family vacation that will create lasting memories. The latter aligns with values of togetherness and experience, offering greater satisfaction. This kind of purposeful allocation is especially crucial when your income isn't steady. If you're a farmer, you might prioritize saving for essential equipment over less critical expenses. For an entrepreneur, marketing costs could take precedence, ensuring that the business continues to thrive even during unpredictable economic shifts. Aligning spending with values not only brings peace of mind but also ensures that every dollar spent contributes to a larger vision for your life.

To start budgeting with purpose, consider setting both short-term and long-term financial goals. Short-term goals might include building an emergency fund or paying off a small debt. Long-term goals could focus on saving for retirement or buying a home. Once these goals are clear, create budget categories that reflect these priorities. Allocate your income in a way that funds these categories first. This might mean cutting back on non-essentials to focus on what truly matters.

Purposeful budgeting leads to greater financial satisfaction and progress. **When you know that your spending is aligned with your values and goals, financial stress diminishes.** This clarity allows you to make confident decisions without second-guessing yourself. The peace of mind that comes from knowing you're on track to meet your goals is invaluable. This approach naturally encourages increased savings for the things that matter most. As you see your financial goals coming to fruition, you build momentum, motivating you to continue on this path. It's a cycle that reinforces itself, where purposeful budgeting begets more purposeful budgeting.

Look at Henry, a young professional who dreamed of owning a home. By setting a clear goal and budget, they were able to save diligently, cutting unnecessary expenses and prioritizing their down payment fund. Over time, this commitment paid off, allowing them to purchase their dream home. Or think of a family dedicated to their children's future education. By aligning their budget with this priority, they gradually built a college fund, ensuring that their kids could pursue higher education without the burden of debt. These examples illustrate the power of allocating every dollar with intention. Each financial decision becomes a step toward achieving meaningful goals.

2.5 The Art of Adjusting: Flexibility in Budgeting

Living with a variable income demands a flexible approach to budgeting. This flexibility is not merely a luxury; it is a necessity. *When your income fluctuates, so must your financial plan.* You may find yourself facing unexpected changes, such as a sudden influx of cash or an unforeseen downturn. Adapting to these shifts without stress requires a budget that can bend without breaking. Consider using rolling averages to better anticipate your financial needs. By calculating an average income over several months, you can smooth out the peaks and valleys, allowing for more consistent planning. This method provides a clearer picture of your typical earnings, which can guide more stable budgeting decisions.

Irregular expenses add another layer of complexity to managing your finances. These might include quarterly taxes, annual insurance premiums, or unexpected car repairs. When these surprise expenses arise, they can throw a rigid budget into disarray. **Building flexibility into your budgeting** allows you to manage these irregularities without unraveling your financial plan. One strategy is to create a buffer within your budget specifically for these expenses. Allocating a small portion of your income each month to a "surprise expenses" fund can provide a cushion when these costs appear. This proactive approach reduces stress and ensures that you can handle unexpected financial demands without derailing your entire budget.

Regular financial reviews are crucial for maintaining flexibility and adapting to changes. A mid-year review, for example, offers an opportunity to assess your progress and make necessary adjustments. This practice involves revisiting your budget, evaluating your spending, and comparing your actual income against your projections. Are you staying within your budget? Have your priorities shifted? These reviews serve as a checkpoint, allowing you to recalibrate your financial plan to better reflect your current situation. They can also highlight areas where you may need to tighten spending or adjust your savings strategy. By taking the time to review and adjust, you maintain control over your financial trajectory, even amidst fluctuations.

For individuals with variable incomes, the ability to pivot and adjust is paramount. Flexibility in budgeting accommodates life's unpredictability, providing stability in an otherwise uncertain financial landscape. Consider the story of a freelance photographer. Some months bring more work than others, with weddings in the summer and holiday events in the winter. By using a flexible budget, they can allocate more funds towards savings during busy months, ensuring they have enough to cover expenses during quieter times. Similarly, a seasonal worker in the tourism industry might use income from the peak season to prepare for the off-season, maintaining a balanced financial state year-round. This adaptive approach empowers you to take charge of your finances, turning variability from a challenge into an opportunity for growth and resilience.

Conducting a Financial Review:

- **Revisit Your Budget**: Check if your budget aligns with your current income and expenses.
- **Evaluate Spending**: Compare your spending habits to your goals and identify areas for improvement.
- **Assess Income vs. Projections**: Review how your actual income matches your expected earnings.
- **Check for Priority Shifts**: Determine if your financial priorities have changed and adjust accordingly.
- **Identify Necessary Adjustments**: Highlight areas where you need to tighten spending or revise your savings plan.

- **Plan for Variability**: For variable incomes, allocate more to savings during high-income periods to cover low-income months.

- **Maintain Flexibility**: Stay adaptable to changes and pivot your financial strategy as needed.

- **Set a Mid-Year Checkpoint**: Conduct a structured review at least once a year to stay on track.

2.6 Navigating Cash Flow: Strategies for Smoothing Income

Cash flow management is the process of tracking how money moves in and out of your accounts. For those with irregular income, it's vital to ensure that your expenses are covered even in low-income periods while planning for future financial needs. Imagine your cash flow as the bloodstream of your financial body. It must be steady and reliable to maintain health. Without it, you might find yourself unable to meet basic obligations or take advantage of future opportunities. Ensuring that you have a clear understanding of your cash flow allows you to plan for months when income might not meet expectations.

One effective technique for smoothing income is setting up a **rolling average**. By calculating an average income over several months, you create a more stable basis for budgeting. This method smooths out the highs and lows, providing a more predictable financial picture. Another strategy we have already established is using savings to compensate for lean months. By setting aside extra funds during high-earning periods, you create a buffer that can cover expenses when income dips. Tools that monitor income trends can also be helpful here. They help you anticipate peak and off-season fluctuations, allowing you to adjust your spending and saving habits accordingly. For example, a musician might use previous gig earnings to project future income, ensuring they're prepared for quieter months.

Maintaining a financial reserve or cushion is crucial. This savings buffer acts as a safety net, absorbing the shock of unpredictable expenses or income shortages. Planning for predictable irregular expenses, like annual subscriptions or insurance premiums, ensures you're not caught off guard. A well-maintained reserve provides peace of mind, knowing you can handle life's surprises without derailing your financial plans. Consider the story of a musician who, by carefully managing their gig earnings and maintaining a reserve, was able to weather a dry spell in bookings without resorting to debt. This stability allowed them to focus on their craft rather than financial stress.

In real life, effective cash flow management can lead to lasting financial stability. Let's look at an example of handling project-based income. By using a rolling average to predict the monthly earnings, we could budget more effectively, setting aside funds during lucrative months to cover times when projects were scarce. This proactive approach ensures that our financial obligations are always met, regardless of income variability. In doing so, we also maintain a reserve for unexpected business expenses, such as travel for a sudden client meeting. These strategies not only provide financial security but also allow us to pursue new opportunities without fear of monetary constraints.

2.7 Overcoming Objections: Making Budgets Work for You

When it comes to budgeting, many people feel resistance. It's a tool often seen as restrictive, a set of shackles that bind your spending rather than freeing you. *The perception is that budgeting tells you what you can't do rather than helping you achieve what you can.* For those with unpredictable income, this sentiment is heightened. The thought of pinning down a budget when your earnings are as changeable as the weather can seem impossible. You might hear that budgeting is irrelevant for those whose paychecks vary so widely. *But let's challenge that notion.* I have a student named Karen who initially resisted the idea of budgeting, but it ultimately transformed her financial situation. Another student, Shannon, is a freelance writer who also feared the limitations of a budget. However, she soon realized that having a financial plan actually gave her more freedom and reduced her stress.

So, how can you overcome these objections and make budgeting a part of your life? **Start by simplifying the process.** A budget doesn't have to be an elaborate spreadsheet with hundreds of categories. It can be as simple as jotting down your main expenses and checking in with them regularly. Flexibility is key; allow yourself some room for unexpected expenses. Consider implementing a "miscellaneous" category for those little surprises that inevitably crop up. **Make sure your budget includes allowances for fun and leisure**, so it doesn't feel like a punishment. This way, you can enjoy the activities you love without guilt or worry. By incorporating flexibility and allowances, you can create a budget that works with your lifestyle, not against it.

Commitment to budgeting brings its own rewards. It increases your awareness and control over your finances, helping you understand where your money goes and why. This newfound clarity can lead to the achievement of financial goals and milestones you once thought impossible. Whether it's saving for a trip, paying off debt, or simply feeling more secure, the benefits of sticking to a budget are tangible. You'll find that the more you engage with your budget, the more confident you become in your financial decisions. It's about building a relationship with your money, one where you are in control rather than feeling at its mercy.

Chapter 3: Debt Management and Reduction Techniques

Debt can often feel like an ever-present shadow looming over your financial landscape. It's easy to become overwhelmed, especially when income is unpredictable. Yet, understanding your debt profile is the first step toward regaining control and moving toward financial freedom. Imagine debt as a puzzle—an intricate combination of pieces that reveal a complete picture of your financial obligations when understood and arranged correctly. Just as each type of debt has distinct characteristics, each piece of your debt puzzle requires a specific approach to manage effectively.

A debt profile is essentially a snapshot of your financial obligations, detailing the types and amounts of debt you owe. Secured debt is typically backed by collateral, like a mortgage or car loan. If you fail to repay, the lender can seize the collateral. On the other hand, unsecured debt includes credit cards and personal loans, which don't involve collateral but often come with higher interest rates due to the increased risk for lenders. Understanding the difference between these types of debt is crucial, as they require different strategies for management and repayment. Interest rates and terms further define your debt profile. These details determine how much you'll ultimately pay over the life of the loan. For individuals with variable incomes, including seasonal earners like farmers or those with steady but fluctuating freelance work, knowing these details can inform better financial decisions.

To thoroughly assess your personal debt situation, start by creating a detailed list of all debts. Include the creditor's name, the outstanding balance, interest rates, minimum monthly payments, and due dates. This comprehensive overview lets you see the full extent of your financial obligations. Once you have this information, calculate your total debt and consider how much you pay each month. This exercise illuminates the path to debt reduction and highlights areas where you can make immediate changes to improve cash flow. Knowing your debt profile helps you identify high-priority debts—those with high interest rates and short terms that can escalate quickly if not addressed. It also aids in planning repayment strategies, allowing you to allocate resources efficiently and make informed decisions about which debts to tackle first.

Several tools and resources can assist in analyzing your debt profile accurately. Online debt calculators are particularly useful, offering insights into how long it will take to pay off debts based on different payment scenarios. Financial planning software, such as Quicken or Mint, provides a comprehensive view of your finances, tracking income, expenses, and debts in one place. These tools simplify the process of managing your debt, allowing you to see the impact of various repayment strategies in real-time. By leveraging technology, you can better understand your financial landscape and make adjustments that align with your goals.

Debt Assessment Checklist

To get started, use this checklist to evaluate your debt profile:

- **List all debts**: Include creditor, balance, interest rate, and monthly payment.

- **Calculate total debt**: Sum all outstanding balances.

- **Identify high-priority debts**: Focus on high-interest and short-term obligations.

- **Choose assessment tools**: Utilize online calculators and financial software.

- **Plan repayment strategies**: Prioritize based on interest rates and terms.

Taking the time to understand your debt profile is an empowering step towards financial stability. It enables you to take control, make informed decisions, and ultimately reduce the stress that debt can cause. As you gain clarity, you'll find that managing debt becomes less about anxiety and more about strategic planning.

3.1 The Debt Avalanche vs. Debt Snowball: Choosing Your Path

When it comes to paying off debt, choosing the right strategy can make all the difference. Two popular methods are the **debt avalanche** and the **debt snowball**. Each approach offers unique benefits, and the choice largely depends on your financial situation and personal preferences. The *debt avalanche method focuses on tackling the debt with the highest interest rate first.* Paying off high-interest debts initially minimizes the amount of interest accumulated over time. This method requires discipline, as it might take longer to see smaller debts disappear. However, the long-term savings on interest payments can be significant, making it an attractive choice for those committed to reducing overall costs.

On the other hand, the *debt snowball method emphasizes paying off the smallest debts first*. This approach is designed to build momentum and motivation by allowing you to see quick wins early in the process. Each time you pay off a debt, no matter how small, you gain a sense of accomplishment that fuels your drive to continue. As you eliminate smaller debts, the payments you used to make on them can be rolled into larger debts, accelerating the process. While the debt snowball method may not save as much on interest as the avalanche, it provides psychological benefits that can be crucial for maintaining motivation.

The pros and cons of each method must be weighed carefully. The **debt avalanche offers faster debt reduction in terms** *of interest savings*, but it demands consistent dedication and might not provide immediate gratification. This method is ideal for financially disciplined people who can handle the slower pace of early progress. Conversely, the **debt snowball can deliver quick psychological boosts**, which can be invaluable if you struggle with staying motivated. It's particularly suitable for those who need to see tangible results to keep going, even if it means paying slightly more in interest over the long run.

Consider the story of Sarah, who chose the debt avalanche method. With several high-interest credit card debts, she decided to tackle the one with the highest rate first. Although it took months to pay off the first debt, the relief and savings were worth it. She eventually cleared all her debts and saved a substantial amount in interest. Meanwhile, Tom opted for the debt snowball approach. With multiple small debts weighing him down, he focused on paying off the smallest first. Each cleared debt boosted his confidence, and he quickly gained the momentum needed to tackle larger ones. Tom found that the sense of achievement kept him motivated throughout the process, leading to a debt-free life.

Both Sarah and Tom illustrate that there is no one-size-fits-all answer to debt reduction. The key is to understand your personal financial behavior and choose a method that aligns with your goals and motivations. Whether you opt for the avalanche or the snowball, the important thing is to stay committed and keep moving forward.

Method	Focus	Ideal For	Key Advantage
Debt Snowball	Smallest balance first	Those seeking quick wins and motivation	Boosts psychological momentum
Debt Avalanche	Highest interest rate	Those prioritizing long-term savings	Minimizes total interest paid over time

3.2 Evaluating Profitability

Understanding the profitability of your endeavors is key, especially when dealing with variable income. For many, the allure of a new venture or side hustle can be enticing, promising both financial gain and personal satisfaction. However, determining whether an endeavor is truly profitable requires careful evaluation of costs, revenue, and potential for growth. Imagine a farmer who decides to start a local produce delivery service. The idea seems promising: fresh, locally sourced produce delivered directly to customers. However, before diving in, the farmer needs to consider various factors. What are the costs of package materials and transportation? How will these expenses impact overall profitability? By analyzing these elements, the farmer can identify whether the delivery service is *a sustainable addition to their operation or merely a drain on resources.*

To evaluate profitability effectively, it's important to assess both direct and indirect costs. Direct costs are those that can be directly attributed to the product or service, such as materials and labor. Indirect costs, on the other hand, include overhead expenses like utilities and rent. By understanding these different cost structures, you can gain a clearer picture of your venture's financial health. Additionally, consider the potential for growth. Is there a demand for your product or service that could lead to increased revenue over time? Are there opportunities to expand your offerings or reach new markets? These factors can significantly influence profitability and should be considered when evaluating your endeavors.

Using financial tools and resources can enhance your ability to assess profitability. Spreadsheets and financial software can help track expenses, revenue, and profit margins, providing valuable insights into your business operations. These tools allow you to visualize your financial data, making it easier to identify trends and make informed decisions. For those less familiar with financial analysis, consulting with a financial advisor or accountant can provide additional guidance and support. They can help you interpret your financial data, identify areas for improvement, and develop strategies to enhance profitability.

Ultimately, evaluating profitability is an ongoing process. It requires regular review and adjustment to ensure that your ventures remain aligned with your financial goals. By staying vigilant and proactive, you can identify areas for improvement, capitalize on opportunities, and make informed decisions that support your long-term financial success. Whether you're a farmer, bartender, or anyone exploring new income streams, understanding profitability is key to transforming your efforts into sustainable financial gains.

3.3 Breaking Free: Psychological Wins in Debt Reduction

The journey of debt reduction is as much a mental endeavor as it is a financial one. The weight of debt often brings with it a heavy emotional burden. Fear, anxiety, and the constant worry about making ends meet can become overwhelming. These emotions not only cloud your judgment but also hinder your ability to make sound financial decisions. Overcoming these psychological barriers is essential. By addressing the fear and anxiety associated with debt, you open the door to a clearer mindset. Building confidence through small victories is a powerful strategy. Each time you make a dent in your debt, celebrate it. Small achievements provide tangible proof that progress is possible, boosting morale and motivation.

To maintain this motivation, it's helpful to employ psychological strategies tailored to your debt reduction journey. Celebrating milestones, no matter how minor, reinforces your commitment. Did you manage to pay off a seasonal equipment loan or clear a credit card balance? Treat yourself to a small reward, reinforcing the positive habit. Visualizing a debt-free future can also serve as a powerful motivator. *Picture yourself free from financial burdens, enjoying the freedom and flexibility that comes with it.* This visualization can serve as a guiding light, keeping you focused and driven even when the path seems daunting.

Setting realistic goals is fundamental to sustaining momentum. These goals should be achievable, providing a steady stream of accomplishments to keep you engaged.

Short-term goals might involve paying off a specific credit card, while long-term goals could focus on eliminating all unsecured debt. Regularly reviewing and adjusting these targets ensures they remain relevant and attainable. As your financial situation evolves, so too should your goals. This flexibility prevents stagnation and keeps your debt reduction efforts aligned with your broader financial aspirations.

Take Cody and Leah for instance, a couple who faced mounting debt anxiety. They initially felt paralyzed by the sheer scale of what they owed. But by breaking their debt into manageable parts and celebrating each small success, they found their anxiety slowly diminished. Each paid-off bill was a step toward financial liberation. Or take Sue, a single parent who, despite juggling multiple responsibilities, set a goal to reduce her debt by a certain percentage each month. By focusing on small, incremental achievements, she gradually chipped away at her debt, gaining confidence with each milestone. These stories exemplify the power of setting achievable targets and celebrating victories, no matter how small.

Incorporating these strategies into your debt reduction plan can transform what might seem an insurmountable challenge into a series of manageable tasks. By acknowledging the psychological aspects of debt, you empower yourself to tackle it head-on. As you celebrate each victory, visualize your progress, and adjust your goals, the path to debt freedom becomes clearer and more attainable.

3.4 Innovative Debt Management Tools and Resources

Choosing the right tool involves considering several factors. Start by evaluating the user interface. A tool should be intuitive and easy to navigate. If you find yourself frustrated with complex features, it won't serve you well in the long run. Look for apps and platforms with comprehensive features that cater to your specific debt-tracking needs. Some might offer detailed analytics, while others focus more on simplicity and ease of use. Consider what aligns best with your financial habits and preferences. Reading reviews and testimonials can provide additional insights. Users often share their experiences, highlighting both the strengths and potential pitfalls of these tools. This feedback can guide your decision, helping you choose a tool that fits seamlessly into your financial routine.

A colleague who is rather tech-savvy shared how using Undebt transformed their approach to debt management. The app's ability to manually track progress and offer multiple payoff plans allowed them to tailor their strategy. The visual representation of their debt reduction journey kept them motivated, and the sense of accomplishment with each milestone was palpable. Another user praised Qoins for its ability to automate payments, effectively reducing their debt without the constant need for manual adjustments. This hands-off approach allowed them to focus on other areas of their financial life, secure in the knowledge that their debts were being managed efficiently.

These stories highlight the transformative power of using the right tools in your debt management strategy. *By leveraging technology, you can create a structured, manageable plan that aligns with your goals.* The convenience and real-time insights offered by these tools make them invaluable assets in the quest for financial freedom. Whether you're a freelancer juggling multiple income streams or a parent managing household finances, these resources can simplify your journey, providing the guidance and support needed to thrive. Find one you like and stick to it!

3.5 Avoiding Debt Traps: Strategies for Long-Term Success

Debt can be like quicksand. You step into it, and before you know it, you're sinking deeper. High-interest credit cards are one of the most common traps, luring you with the promise of instant gratification. The thrill of buying now and paying later often blinds you to the long-term consequences. Interest rates can climb into the double digits, and if you're only making minimum payments, it's like pouring water into a bucket with a hole at the bottom—it never fills. Loans with unfavorable terms present another challenge. They might have seemed manageable at first, but over time, they can balloon into burdensome debt. Impulsive spending habits further complicate matters, especially when they become a pattern. It's easy to swipe your card for small purchases, thinking they won't add up. But they do. And for freelancers or those with irregular income, payday loans might feel like a lifeline. However, the short repayment terms and exorbitant fees can trap you in a cycle that's hard to escape.

To steer clear of these pitfalls, you need a strategy. Establishing a strict budget for discretionary spending is a must here. By defining your financial boundaries, you can make thoughtful decisions about where your money goes. Regularly reviewing your financial statements also plays a vital role. This practice helps you spot trends, understand your spending habits, and make necessary adjustments. It's like checking the map on a road trip to ensure you're headed in the right direction. And building your emergency fund is another powerful tool in your arsenal. Automated savings plans can assist in transferring funds to your savings account without you having to think about it. This way, when emergencies arise, you're prepared and less likely to resort to debt.

Avoid falling into the debt traps we are all faced with. Take Ashley, a recent college grad with a great fist job who learned a hard lesson with credit card debt. Initially, she viewed her credit card as a kind of free money, spending without much thought. But soon, the monthly statements piled up, and the interest compounded. Realizing the gravity of her situation, she created a budget and prioritized repayment. Slowly but surely, she chipped away at the debt, learning to live within her means. Or think of Megan's family who faced medical debt. An unexpected illness led to significant expenses, and without an emergency fund, they turned to credit. The debt ballooned, causing stress until they sought help. By renegotiating terms and tightening their budget, they managed to regain control. These cautionary tales underscore the importance of vigilance and preparation. Without a plan, it's easy to fall into debt traps. But with discipline and foresight, you can navigate the financial landscape with confidence.

3.6 Rebuilding Credit: Steps to Improve Your Financial Health

Credit health isn't just a number; it's a key that unlocks opportunities. A good credit score can be the difference between securing a loan with favorable terms and being burdened with high interest rates that eat away at your finances. It's about having the power to negotiate better deals, whether you're buying a car, applying for a mortgage, or even getting a new phone plan. In a world where financial stability often hinges on access to credit, maintaining a healthy score becomes vital. Lower interest rates on future credit mean you pay less over time, allowing your money to work harder for you. A strong credit score can also be a safety net, offering you options when unexpected expenses arise.

Improving your credit score is a process that requires patience and diligence. Start by paying your bills on time—every time. Consistency is critical. Even small missed payments can significantly impact your score, so setting up automatic payments or reminders can be a lifesaver. Reducing credit card balances is another effective step. Aim to keep your credit utilization below 30% of your total available credit. This demonstrates to lenders that you're not overly reliant on borrowed money, which can improve your score over time. If you have multiple credit cards, paying down those with the highest balances first can also provide a boost.

Credit monitoring services are great tools in your arsenal. They help keep track of your credit score and provide alerts for any changes, allowing you to catch potential issues early. Many services offer free access to your credit report, which you should review at least annually. Look for errors or discrepancies, as these can unjustly lower your score. If you find any, *dispute them promptly*. Regular monitoring also helps protect against fraud, as you'll be notified of any suspicious activity on your accounts. By staying informed, you can take swift action to safeguard your credit health.

Michael faced the daunting task of rebuilding his credit after bankruptcy. It wasn't easy, but through consistent effort, he managed to turn things around. By focusing on paying bills punctually and gradually reducing his debt, he saw steady improvements in his score. He used a credit monitoring service to track his progress and stay motivated. Similarly, Lisa found herself with a low credit score due to overspending in her early twenties. Determined to improve her financial future, she developed a plan to pay down her debts and used her tax refunds strategically to make larger payments. Over time, her credit score rose, opening new doors for her.

Rebuilding credit is about taking small, consistent steps that add up to significant change. It's not just about numbers; it's about forging a path to greater financial freedom and stability. As you focus on improving your credit, remember that every positive action brings you closer to your goals. You have the power to shape your financial future, one payment and one decision at a time.

Chapter 4: Building and Maintaining an Emergency Fund

Imagine standing on shifting sands, where each step forward feels uncertain, and the ground beneath is never quite solid. This is the reality for many living with a variable income, where the financial landscape constantly changes, and the unexpected is a given. In such a world, an emergency fund is not just a safety net; it is your anchor, providing stability when everything else wavers. An emergency fund serves as a financial buffer against life's unpredictable moments. It is there to catch you when expenses arise that you didn't see coming—a sudden car repair, an unexpected medical bill, or even a temporary drop in income. For those with fluctuating earnings, this fund is crucial. It allows you to manage these surprises without derailing your long-term financial plans or resorting to high-interest credit solutions.

For individuals with irregular income streams, the need for a robust safety net is even more pronounced. When your paycheck varies from month to month, planning becomes a game of balancing on a tightrope. During lean months, when income gaps loom large, having an emergency fund can mean the difference between staying afloat and falling into debt. It is your financial lifeline, bridging the gap between what you earn and what you need. This cushion not only supports you during the troughs but also empowers you to take calculated risks, knowing that you have a fallback. Whether you're a freelancer awaiting a delayed payment or an entrepreneur investing in a new venture, an emergency fund provides the security to navigate these challenges with confidence.

The psychological benefits of having an emergency fund cannot be overstated. Financial stress is a pervasive anxiety that creeps into every aspect of life, affecting your mental health and personal relationships. But when you know you have a financial cushion, that stress diminishes. It gives you peace of mind, freeing your mental bandwidth to focus on other priorities, be it your career, family, or personal growth. The knowledge that you can handle financial hiccups without panic fosters a sense of empowerment and control. Instead of reacting in crisis mode, you can plan proactively, making decisions based on your goals rather than immediate needs.

Consider the story of Jamie, a freelance graphic designer who faced an unforeseen medical emergency. Without an emergency fund, the cost of treatment could have spiraled into unaffordable debt. However, having saved diligently during higher-earning months, Jamie was able to cover the expenses without financial distress. This foresight not only preserved Jamie's financial health but also allowed for recovery without the added burden of financial anxiety. Similarly, Alex, a gig worker reliant on unpredictable ride-share earnings, experienced a major car breakdown. The repair costs threatened to sideline income entirely. Yet, Alex's emergency fund—painstakingly built over time—provided the means to cover the repairs promptly, ensuring a swift return to work and income generation. These stories underscore the tangible impact of having a financial safety net.

Building Your Emergency Fund

1. **Calculate Monthly Fixed Expenses:** Determine the amount needed to cover essential costs each month (e.g., rent, utilities, insurance).
2. **Set a Savings Goal:** Decide how many months of expenses your reserve should cover (e.g., 3–6 months).
3. **Identify Peak Income Periods:** Pinpoint months when income is highest and commit to saving more during these times.
4. **Open a Separate Savings Account:** Keep your cash reserve separate to avoid accidental spending.
5. **Automate Savings:** Schedule automatic transfers during peak income months to build your reserve consistently.
6. **Monitor Progress:** Regularly check your reserve balance and adjust contributions as needed.
7. **Replenish After Use:** If you dip into the reserve, prioritize rebuilding it during the next high-income period.

Incorporating these steps into your financial routine can set the foundation for a resilient financial future. *An emergency fund is more than an account with money; it is a testament to foresight and discipline, a tangible measure of your commitment to financial stability.* As you build this fund, you are not just saving money; you are constructing a fortress of security that shields you from the unpredictability of life, allowing you to pursue your goals with confidence and peace.

4.1 Small Steps, Big Impact: Starting Your Savings Journey

Beginning your savings journey can feel daunting, especially when your income doesn't follow a predictable path. But here's the thing: you don't need to start big to make a significant impact. Small, consistent steps can set you on the path to financial security. Consider setting a manageable goal, like saving $10 a week. It might not seem like much at first glance, but over time, these small savings accumulate and grow. This approach is particularly useful for bartenders who face slower seasons. During busier times, setting aside a modest amount each week can create a buffer for those quieter months. *The key is consistency, building a habit that becomes second nature.*

The beauty of small contributions lies in the power of compounding savings. When you regularly set aside a portion of your income, even if it's from the change left over after buying groceries, you're allowing your money to grow. Over time, these contributions add up significantly. Imagine a savings growth chart that starts with a small line, gradually rising over the months. As the months pass, that line begins to curve upward, representing the compound growth of your efforts. It's a visual reminder that even humble beginnings can lead to substantial outcomes. The principle of compounding is simple yet powerful, turning your regular contributions into a sizeable fund over time. This growth can offer the financial security you need to face unexpected expenses without stress.

Maintaining regular contributions requires a strategic approach, especially when your income is tight. Automated transfers can be your ally here. By setting up a system that automatically moves a set amount into your savings account each week or month, you remove the temptation to skip a contribution. This automation ensures that saving becomes a consistent part of your financial routine. Spare change apps like Acorns can also play a role. They round up your everyday purchases to the nearest dollar and invest the difference. It's a seamless way to grow your savings without feeling the pinch. These strategies help you maintain the momentum needed to build your emergency fund steadily.

Real-life stories often serve as the best motivation. Take the example of Taylor who set out to build a $1,000 emergency fund. At first, the goal seemed overwhelming. But by committing to saving just $15 every week, they gradually chipped away at their target. Over time, they watched their savings grow, motivated by each small milestone. This sense of achievement bolstered their confidence, encouraging them to continue saving even after reaching their initial goal. Their story is a testament to the power of setting achievable targets and sticking to them, no matter how modest they might seem at the start.

These small steps might feel insignificant in isolation, but together, they create a solid foundation for financial resilience. By starting small and building momentum, you're not just saving money; you're cultivating a habit that supports your financial well-being. Each contribution brings you closer to a more secure future, one that offers peace of mind and the freedom to focus on what truly matters. The journey of building an emergency fund is not about grand gestures but about the steady, consistent effort that leads to long-term stability.

4.2 Finding Hidden Savings: Unearthing Opportunities

In our daily hustle, it's easy to overlook the small expenses that quietly drain our wallets. But even subtle changes can lead to substantial savings over time. Start by examining common expense categories that often get overlooked. Subscription services, for instance, can add up quickly. Whether it's video streaming, magazines, or meal kits, these monthly charges often go unnoticed, yet they steadily chip away at your budget. Consider auditing your subscriptions. Are you using all of them regularly, or are there a few that could be paused or canceled? The same scrutiny should apply to dining out and entertainment costs. It's all too easy to grab a quick coffee or plan a spontaneous dinner out. While these activities bring joy, they can also become habitual expenses that prevent you from building your emergency fund. By reducing these splurges, you will likely find a bit more breathing room in your finances.

Mindful spending is another powerful tool in your financial toolkit. It encourages you to critically evaluate your spending habits, prompting you to ask whether each purchase aligns with your priorities and values.

A spending journal can be useful in this process. By recording every purchase, you gain a clear view of where your money goes. This practice isn't about restricting yourself but about creating awareness.

Over time, you'll start to notice patterns—perhaps you spend more on takeout during busy weeks or indulge in retail therapy when stressed. Recognizing these tendencies enables you to make intentional choices about where to cut back. You might decide to cook more meals at home or set a monthly budget for treats, allowing you to enjoy them guilt-free.

To assist in tracking expenses, technology offers several useful tools. Apps like PocketGuard can simplify the process, helping you identify unnecessary spending with ease. These apps sync with your bank accounts, providing a real-time snapshot of your finances. They categorize expenses, flagging areas where you're overspending and suggesting practical adjustments. This digital approach makes it easier to stay on top of your financial habits, offering insights that a traditional spreadsheet might miss. By using these tools, you can set realistic goals and monitor your progress, ensuring that your savings efforts remain on track.

4.3 Reflection Section: Uncover Your Savings

- **Audit Your Subscriptions**: List all recurring subscriptions. Decide which ones to keep, pause, or cancel.

- **Monitor Dining and Entertainment**: Track how often you dine out or indulge in entertainment. Consider setting a monthly limit.

- **Start a Spending Journal**: For one month, record every purchase. Identify patterns and areas for improvement.

- **Utilize Expense Tracking Apps**: Choose an app like PocketGuard to help categorize and analyze spending.

These strategies and tools can transform the way you manage your finances, revealing hidden savings that contribute to your emergency fund. By focusing on mindful spending and leveraging technology, you can optimize your budget, ensuring that each dollar works toward your financial goals. Through small, deliberate changes, you lay the groundwork for a more stable and secure future.

4.4 Protecting Your Fund: Strategies to Avoid Dipping In

The emergency fund you've worked so hard to build is your financial fortress, designed to protect you from life's unexpected challenges. It's crucial to keep this fund intact for genuine emergencies—those unforeseen, unavoidable events that could otherwise send your financial stability into a tailspin. Differentiating between wants and needs is the first step in safeguarding this fund. *Needs are the essentials*: housing, utilities, and food. *Wants, on the other hand, are those discretionary pleasures* that, while enjoyable, aren't vital to your day-to-day survival. By clearly distinguishing between these categories, you can ensure that you reserve your emergency fund for moments that truly require it rather than dipping into it for non-essential spending.

Maintaining discipline in managing your emergency fund requires setting clear rules for its use. This means establishing a set of criteria that define what constitutes an emergency. For instance, a job loss or major medical expense may qualify, whereas a sale at your favorite store does not. By having these guidelines in place, you reduce the temptation to use the fund for non-emergencies. Another effective strategy is implementing a "pause" period before making any withdrawals. When faced with a potential expense, wait a few days to assess whether it's truly necessary. This pause allows emotions to settle and provides time for rational decision-making, often revealing that the urgency of the expense was overestimated.

There are alternative solutions for handling financial needs without tapping into your emergency fund. *Consider creating a separate savings account specifically for planned expenses, such as holidays, birthdays, or anticipated home repairs.* This account acts as a buffer, ensuring that your emergency fund remains untouched for genuine crises. Exploring low-interest credit options can also provide temporary relief for cash flow issues, allowing you to address immediate needs without depleting your savings. While credit should be used judiciously, it can serve as a stopgap measure when managed carefully. It's essential to weigh the costs and benefits, ensuring that any borrowed funds can be repaid promptly to avoid accruing debt.

We can see the importance of these strategies when we take a look at examples from people like Dean, a single parent who faced the challenge of maintaining savings while managing household expenses. By applying strict rules for fund usage, Dean successfully navigated financial tight spots without depleting their emergency fund. During a particularly tough month, when unexpected school expenses arose, Dean used their separate savings account to cover the costs, leaving the emergency fund untouched. This foresight and discipline paid off when a true emergency—a sudden medical bill—required immediate attention. Having preserved the fund, Dean was able to meet this expense head-on without financial strain.

These disciplined approaches to fund management are not just about preserving money; they are about preserving your peace of mind and financial future. By setting boundaries, exploring alternatives, and maintaining discipline, you can ensure that your emergency fund remains a steadfast ally in times of need. It serves as a testament to your commitment to financial health, providing a cushion that allows you to face life's uncertainties with confidence and resilience.

4.5 Creative Ways to Boost Your Emergency Savings

Building an emergency fund doesn't always have to follow the traditional path of setting aside a fixed amount regularly. Sometimes, thinking outside the box can lead to unexpected savings. One innovative method is participating in savings challenges. These are not just about stashing away cash; they turn saving into a game, infusing it with a sense of fun and competition. For example, the 52-week challenge encourages you to save an increasing amount each week for a year. Start with $1 in the first week, $2 in the second, and so on until you reach $52 in the last week. By the end, you'll have accumulated a substantial amount without feeling the pinch. Another popular challenge is the "no-spend month," where you commit to spending only on essentials, funneling what you save directly into your emergency fund. These challenges can instill discipline and make saving a communal activity if done with friends or family.

Another straightforward yet effective strategy is selling unused items online. Most of us have belongings collecting dust—clothes, electronics, or furniture—that could be turned into cash. Platforms like eBay, Craigslist, or Facebook Marketplace make it easy to reach potential buyers. This approach not only declutters your space but also provides a quick influx of money that can be directed straight into your savings. It's surprising how much value is hidden in items you no longer need. For example, a set of old textbooks or a vintage jacket can fetch more than you might expect. By setting aside a weekend to sort through your belongings, you might find a treasure trove of opportunities to boost your savings.

Exploring additional income opportunities is another effective way to bolster your emergency fund. The gig economy offers a wealth of options to suit various skills and interests. Freelancing on platforms like Upwork or Fiverr allows you to monetize your talents, whether it's writing, graphic design, or coding. For those who enjoy teaching, online tutoring services like VIPKid or Tutor.com provide a platform to connect with students globally. These gigs can fit into your schedule, offering flexibility and the chance to earn extra cash when you need it most. Seasonal side hustles are also worth considering. If you're a gig worker with fluctuating demands, you might explore opportunities like pet-sitting during the holidays or working at a local festival. These roles often require short-term commitments but can make a significant impact on your savings. You can really get creative here. I knew someone who worked the summers in West Virginia as a river rafting guide and then would head to Colorado to work as a ski instructor in the winter. Seasonality can have many upsides.

Technology further enhances your ability to save creatively. Cash-back apps like Rakuten can turn everyday purchases into savings opportunities. By using these apps, you earn a percentage back on what you spend. It's a simple way to add to your emergency fund without any additional effort. Over time, these small rewards accumulate, providing a nice bonus to your savings. Additionally, apps that round up your purchases to the nearest dollar and deposit the change into a savings account can help you save without thinking about it. This method leverages the power of small, incremental contributions to gradually build your fund.

As you explore these strategies, remember that the goal is to find what works best for you. Saving doesn't have to be a chore; it can be an enjoyable and rewarding process. By embracing unconventional methods and leveraging technology, you open up new avenues to grow your emergency fund efficiently. What's important is to take action, experiment with different approaches, and remain consistent. Through these creative strategies, you can build a robust financial cushion, offering peace of mind and security.

With your emergency savings strategy strengthened, we turn next to long-term financial planning. It's time to explore how to use these foundations to build lasting wealth and security.

Chapter 5: Strategic Savings and Investment Planning

As the sun sets over a bustling city skyline, the lights flicker on, illuminating the path to financial independence. Whether you're a young professional navigating a fluctuating income, a single parent balancing responsibilities, or an entrepreneur juggling opportunities, this chapter is your guide to mastering savings and investments. By setting realistic goals, exploring tailored strategies, and embracing diversification, you'll build a foundation of financial security and flexibility.

Setting realistic savings goals is the cornerstone of financial success and stability. When goals are too lofty or vague, they become a source of frustration rather than motivation. It's like climbing a mountain without a clear path; you might find yourself discouraged before you even begin. On the other hand, realistic goals provide a tangible target, allowing you to track progress and celebrate small victories along the way. These achievable milestones build confidence, fostering a sense of accomplishment that fuels continued effort. Imagine the satisfaction of reaching a savings benchmark you've set, knowing each step has brought you closer to your ultimate financial destination.

To set effective savings goals, consider employing the SMART criteria: Specific, Measurable, Achievable, Relevant, and Time-bound. This framework transforms abstract aspirations into actionable plans. Start by defining your goals clearly; for instance, "Save $5,000 for a family vacation by next summer" is more effective than "Save money for travel." Ensure your goals are measurable, allowing you to track progress. Achievability is key; set expectations that challenge yet remain within reach. Align your goals with personal values and life aspirations, ensuring they hold genuine significance. Finally, establish a timeline to maintain focus and accountability. By applying this structured approach, you create a roadmap that guides your savings journey with clarity and purpose.

Visualization plays a crucial role in goal achievement. By imagining your goals vividly, you enhance your commitment and motivation. Creating a vision board can serve as a powerful tool, providing a visual representation of your aspirations. Gather images, words, and symbols that resonate with your financial objectives and arrange them on a board. Place it somewhere you'll see daily, keeping your goals front and center. This constant reminder reinforces your dedication, turning dreams into tangible targets. Visualization transforms abstract desires into concrete plans, bridging the gap between intention and action.

Rachel and her family are a determined group with a dream of traveling the world. They set a goal to save for an around-the-world trip, using the SMART criteria to guide their efforts. By breaking their goal into manageable steps, they consistently saved each month and celebrated each milestone along the way. Their vision board, decorated with images of exotic places and beloved destinations, kept them motivated. As their savings grew, so did their excitement, culminating in a journey that fulfilled their dreams. Similarly, Justin and his partner were eager to buy their first home and set a goal to save for a down payment. By aligning their goal with their values of stability and independence, they remained committed, finding creative ways to increase savings. Their dedication paid off, turning the dream of homeownership into reality. These narratives illustrate the transformative power of setting and achieving savings goals, offering a beacon of hope and inspiration.

Creating Your Vision Board

- **Collect Materials**: Gather magazines, photos, and printouts that represent your financial goals.
- **Select Images and Words**: Choose visuals and words that resonate with your aspirations.
- **Arrange on a Board**: Organize your selections on a board, creating a meaningful collage.
- **Display Prominently**: Place your vision board where you'll see it daily to reinforce motivation.
- **Reflect and Adjust**: Regularly revisit and update your board as your goals evolve.

Setting realistic, inspiring savings goals is about more than accumulating wealth; it's about creating a future that aligns with your dreams and values. With clear intentions and a structured approach, you can navigate the complexities of financial planning, turning aspirations into achievements. Whether you're saving for a dream trip, a new home, or future security, the journey of reaching your goals begins with that first step.

5.1 Introduction to Investment: Where to Begin

Investing might seem like a daunting concept, especially if you're new to the financial world. However, starting with the basics can demystify this crucial aspect of financial planning. At its core, investing is about putting your money to work to generate more money over time. Traditional investment options include stocks, bonds, mutual funds, and exchange-traded funds (ETFs):

- **Stocks** represent ownership in a company and can offer high returns, albeit with higher risk.
- **Bonds** are loans to a company or government, providing regular interest payments, and are generally considered safer than stocks.
- **Mutual funds** pool money from many investors to purchase a diversified portfolio of stocks and bonds managed by a professional.
- **ETFs** are similar but trade on exchanges like stocks, offering both diversification and flexibility.

Mutual funds tailored for unpredictable contributions can be a smart choice for those with irregular incomes. They allow you to invest when you can without committing yourself to a fixed schedule.

Starting Early: The Power of Compound Interest

Starting early with investments offers significant advantages, even if you can only contribute small amounts initially. The power of compound interest means that the money you invest earns interest, which in turn earns more interest, leading to exponential growth over time. This principle is the foundation of long-term wealth accumulation. The earlier you start, the more time your investments have to grow. Even modest contributions can lead to substantial savings over decades. For instance, investing $100 a month at a 7% annual return can grow to over $120,000 in 30 years. This growth highlights why starting early matters—it allows your investments to weather market fluctuations and take full advantage of compounding.

Building a Portfolio with Purpose

Creating a portfolio doesn't require vast knowledge or large sums of money—it starts with small, intentional steps:

1. **Define Your Goals**: Clarify what you're investing for—retirement, a home, or education. The clearer your goals, the better your investment choices will align.

2. **Assess Risk Tolerance**: Determine how much risk you can handle without derailing your plan, especially during income fluctuations.

3. **Start Small and Stay Flexible**: Begin with low-cost options like index funds or ETFs, which require minimal investment and offer diversification.

4. **Diversify Thoughtfully**: Spread your investments across asset classes (stocks, bonds, ETFs) to protect against market ups and downs.

5. **Monitor Progress and Rebalance**: Review your portfolio regularly to ensure it reflects your evolving goals and financial situation. Adjust allocations when needed to stay on track.

For those with irregular income, tools like dollar-cost averaging (investing consistent amounts over time) or micro-investing platforms can make investing more accessible. These strategies allow you to invest during peak income periods without locking you into a rigid schedule.

Beginner-Friendly Investment Platforms

For those new to investing, the world of stocks, bonds, and mutual funds can feel intimidating. Beginner-friendly platforms like **Robinhood** and **Acorns** simplify the process, making investing accessible even for those with limited experience or irregular income.

- **Robinhood**: Known for its user-friendly interface and commission-free trading, Robinhood allows you to buy and sell stocks, ETFs, and cryptocurrencies with ease. It's a great option for those looking to get started with direct investments and learn as they go. The platform also offers educational resources and tools to help beginners understand market trends.

- **Acorns**: Perfect for those who want to automate their investments, Acorns rounds up your everyday purchases to the nearest dollar and invests the spare change into diversified portfolios. This micro-investing approach makes it easy to start with small amounts, gradually building wealth over time. Acorns also includes features like retirement accounts and educational content tailored for novice investors.

These platforms are designed to lower the barrier to entry for investing, enabling you to begin your journey with minimal upfront costs and guidance along the way.

Cautionary Note: The Risks of Investing and Diversification

While investing is a powerful tool for building wealth, it's important to approach it with caution. Every investment carries some level of risk, and understanding these risks is essential to making informed decisions.

- **Market Volatility**: The value of investments can fluctuate due to changes in the market, and it's not uncommon for stocks or ETFs to experience short-term losses. This unpredictability can be stressful for irregular income earners if you rely on invested funds for immediate needs.

- **The Importance of Diversification**: Diversification involves spreading your investments across various asset classes (e.g., stocks, bonds, real estate) to minimize the impact of a poor-performing asset. Diversifying reduces the risk of significant losses and creates a more stable portfolio. For example, if the stock market takes a downturn, your bonds or other fixed-income investments may offset some of the losses.

- **Know Your Risk Tolerance**: Assess how much risk you're comfortable taking on before investing. Platforms like Robinhood and Acorns allow you to tailor your investment strategy to align with your risk tolerance, offering options from conservative to aggressive portfolios.

Finally, remember that investing is a long-term strategy. Avoid making impulsive decisions based on market trends or emotions, and consider consulting a financial advisor if you're uncertain about your investment choices.

5.2 Diversifying Income Streams: Building Passive Income

In today's ever-changing economic landscape, relying on a single income source can be risky. Diversifying income streams isn't just a strategy—it's a necessity for financial security and stability. By spreading your financial roots across multiple channels, you reduce the risk of a single setback disrupting your entire financial well-being. This approach offers a safety net, flexibility, and growth opportunities. Imagine balancing a steady job with side hustles or investments that generate passive income. This setup reduces reliance on one paycheck and opens doors to financial freedom.

Exploring passive income avenues can transform your financial landscape. Real estate investments, for instance, offer a time-tested path to passive income. Whether through rental properties or real estate investment trusts (REITs), the potential for consistent earnings is significant. Dividend-paying stocks are another option, providing regular income through profit sharing. For the digitally inclined, creating and selling digital products like ebooks, online courses, or software can build a stream of revenue that requires minimal ongoing effort once established. These opportunities leverage your skills and interests, allowing you to earn while focusing on other priorities.

To embark on building passive income, start with thorough market research. Identify viable opportunities by analyzing trends, demands, and potential returns. This research helps you choose avenues that align with your goals and risk tolerance. Once identified, setting up automated systems is key. For instance, investing in dividend stocks can be automated through brokerage accounts, ensuring reinvestment of earnings. Similarly, digital platforms can automate product sales, managing transactions and deliveries seamlessly. These systems free up time, letting you focus on growth without constant oversight.

Analyzing Trends, Demands, and Potential Returns

The success of any income diversification strategy hinges on thorough research. Here's how to evaluate opportunities effectively:

1. **Understand Market Trends**:
    - Study the trajectory of industries or markets. For example, renewable energy and online education are growing sectors.
    - Analyze how societal or economic changes (e.g., remote work trends, sustainability efforts) influence demand.
2. **Identify Consumer Demand**:
    - Look for gaps in the market or underserved audiences.
    - Use tools like Google Trends, social media platforms, or keyword research to assess the popularity of topics or products.
3. **Evaluate Potential Returns**:
    - Assess the revenue potential by comparing upfront costs to expected income.
    - For investments like real estate or dividend stocks, calculate return on investment (ROI) and compare it to other opportunities.
    - Use online calculators or consult financial advisors for deeper insights.
4. **Match Opportunities with Your Skills and Resources**:
    - Choose income streams that align with your interests, expertise, and available capital.
    - For instance, if you're skilled in graphic design, creating and selling templates may be a low-cost, high-reward option.
5. **Analyze Risk Tolerance**:
    - Consider how much risk you can afford to take. High-risk opportunities, like starting a new business or investing in cryptocurrencies, may not suit everyone.

Setting Up Automated Systems for Passive Income

Once you identify viable opportunities, automation can streamline your efforts:

- **Investments**: Use brokerage accounts to automate dividend reinvestments or schedule recurring contributions to ETFs or mutual funds.
- **Digital Products**: Platforms like Gumroad or Etsy handle transactions and deliveries for ebooks, printables, or other digital assets.
- **Real Estate**: Property management software or professional managers can reduce the hands-on workload for rental properties.

Automation minimizes the time and energy required to maintain your income streams, allowing you to focus on scaling or pursuing additional opportunities.

Building Your Financial Future

Diversifying income streams empowers you to turn variability into opportunity. Whether it's launching a side hustle, investing in assets, or leveraging digital platforms, these strategies create resilience against economic unpredictability. Start small, analyze opportunities carefully, and remain flexible to adapt to changing circumstances.

While this section provides an overview, there are countless resources to deepen your understanding. Explore books like "Rich Dad Poor Dad" for inspiration or The Simple Path to Wealth by JL Collins for practical advice. Online platforms such as Skillshare, Udemy, and Coursera offer courses on topics ranging from digital product creation to real estate investing. By continually learning and experimenting, you can build a financial foundation that supports your goals and grows with you.

5.3 Retirement Planning for Irregular Earners

Navigating retirement planning when your income isn't consistent can feel like trying to map out a journey on shifting sands. For those who earn irregularly—whether freelancers, small business owners, or gig workers—the absence of employer-sponsored retirement plans presents a unique challenge. Unlike traditional employees who might have access to a 401(k) with employer matching, you're often left to forge your own path. This can lead to inconsistent contributions to retirement savings, as the ebb and flow of income make it difficult to maintain a steady saving habit. During high-income months, the temptation might be to save aggressively, but leaner times could force you to dip into those savings just to get by. This lack of consistency can hinder the growth of your retirement fund, making it essential to adopt strategies that cater specifically to variable income earners.

One effective approach is to utilize Individual Retirement Accounts (IRAs), which offer tax advantages and flexibility. Traditional IRAs allow you to contribute pre-tax dollars, reducing taxable income, while Roth IRAs provide tax-free growth on after-tax contributions. For self-employed individuals, options like SEP IRAs and Solo 401(k)s can be particularly beneficial. These plans offer higher contribution limits than standard IRAs, allowing you to save more during prosperous months. A Solo 401(k), for instance, lets you contribute both as an employer and employee, maximizing your savings potential (ForUsAll, n.d.). Exploring these self-employed retirement plans can provide a structured way to build your retirement fund despite the unpredictability of your income.

Seeking the guidance of a financial advisor can significantly enhance your retirement planning process. A certified financial planner brings expertise and objectivity, helping you craft a personalized strategy that aligns with your unique circumstances and goals. They can assist in evaluating your risk tolerance, choosing the right retirement accounts, and determining optimal contribution amounts, even when your income varies. Working with a professional can also provide peace of mind, knowing you have a well-thought-out plan in place. They can offer insights into tax-saving strategies and investment opportunities that you might not have considered on your own. This expert guidance can be invaluable, particularly for those navigating the complexities of retirement planning without a steady paycheck.

Consider the story of a small business owner who faced the daunting task of preparing for retirement without a traditional safety net. By consulting with a financial advisor, they were able to set up a Solo 401(k), taking advantage of its flexibility and higher contribution limits. This allowed them to save efficiently, adapting their contributions based on their business's fluctuating revenue. Similarly, a freelance writer, aware of the challenges posed by variable income, took proactive steps early in their career. They consistently contributed to a Roth IRA, taking advantage of its tax-free growth. Over time, these strategic contributions built a robust retirement fund, ensuring financial security in their later years. These examples demonstrate that with the right tools, planning, and support, irregular earners can successfully navigate the path to a secure retirement.

5.4 Future-Proofing Finances: Embracing Emerging Trends

In an ever-evolving financial landscape, staying ahead requires a willingness to adapt and embrace new trends and technologies. One significant development reshaping personal finance is the rise of sustainable and ethical investing. Investors are increasingly seeking opportunities aligning with their values, focusing on companies prioritizing environmental sustainability, social responsibility, and ethical governance. This shift reflects a broader societal trend toward conscious consumerism, where financial choices reflect personal ethics. For many, this means investing in green energy, sustainable agriculture, or companies with transparent labor practices. These investments not only offer potential financial returns but also contribute to positive global change, aligning with a desire to make a difference.

Adapting to change is crucial in an unpredictable world. Financial strategies that worked yesterday may not be effective tomorrow.

Continuous learning and flexibility are essential to staying informed and making sound decisions. This might involve attending webinars, reading financial news, or engaging with online courses to build your knowledge base. By staying informed, you equip yourself with the tools to navigate shifts in the market landscape. This adaptability ensures you're ready to pivot your strategies when necessary, maintaining your financial health amidst uncertainty. Embracing change doesn't mean abandoning tried-and-true methods; it means augmenting them with innovative approaches that reflect current realities.

To future-proof your finances, consider diversifying your investments to include innovative sectors. The digital age has ushered in many new opportunities, from tech startups to renewable energy projects. By allocating a portion of your portfolio to these emerging industries, you position yourself to benefit from growth trends. Incorporating digital finance tools can also enhance your financial strategy. Platforms that offer automated investing, real-time market analysis, and personalized recommendations can streamline your decision-making process, saving time and increasing efficiency. These tools provide insights that enable you to make informed choices, ensuring your investments align with your goals and risk tolerance.

Consider the story of Michael, an early cryptocurrency adopter. Initially skeptical about the idea of digital currencies, he decided to dive deep into research, dedicating time to understanding blockchain technology and its potential applications. After months of study, he cautiously invested in Bitcoin during its early days. Over time, as the cryptocurrency market grew, so did the value of his investment. Michael's willingness to take an informed risk in this new financial frontier paid off significantly, highlighting the rewards of calculated bravery.

On the other hand, Elena, a socially conscious investor, turned her focus to green energy funds. Passionate about sustainability, she sought out investments in companies prioritizing renewable energy and environmental stewardship. As global demand for clean energy increased, the value of her investments surged, reflecting the growth of this vital industry. Elena's success showcases the potential of aligning financial choices with global trends and personal values.

Michael and Elena's stories demonstrate that embracing emerging opportunities requires a combination of diligence, courage, and adaptability. By staying informed and open to innovation, you too can position yourself to seize opportunities and thrive in a changing financial landscape.

Financial success is not a destination but a journey shaped by informed decisions, persistence, and adaptability. By setting clear savings goals, investing intentionally, diversifying income streams, and planning for the long term, you build resilience against uncertainty.

Your financial journey begins with a single step—whether setting up an automated savings plan, exploring investment opportunities, or taking a course to expand your knowledge. Each action brings you closer to the financial freedom and stability you deserve.

Make a Difference with Your Review

> *"Wealth consists not in having great possessions, but in having few wants."*
> – Epictetus

When we take a moment to share our experiences, we have the opportunity to create a ripple effect that helps others achieve their goals. If I've succeeded in helping you along your financial journey so far, I'd love to ask for your help in return.

Let me explain.

Imagine someone who is just like you—or maybe, like you used to be. They're navigating the stress of unpredictable income, searching for answers, and hoping to find the right tools to take control of their finances. That person might stumble across this book, unsure if it's the right fit for their needs.

Now, imagine this: your review is what helps them make that choice.

Every review has the power to make a difference. For someone managing a variable income, finding a book that offers clarity and solutions can be life-changing. That's why I'm reaching out to you with this simple request:

Will you take 60 seconds to leave a review?

Your review might be the reason someone takes the leap to:

- Build their first-ever budget and feel in control.
- Save consistently for the future they deserve.
- Stop worrying about unexpected expenses.
- Finally grow their wealth and achieve financial stability.
- Gain confidence in managing their money, no matter how unpredictable their income may be.

Your words can inspire someone else to take action. And for that, I'd be incredibly grateful.

Simply click below or scan the QR code to leave your review:

Leave Your Review Here

or scan:

If you're the kind of person who feels good about helping someone you've never met, welcome to the club. Your kindness makes you a part of a community that believes in lifting each other up.

Thank you for making this book—and this mission—even more impactful. I'm thrilled to continue sharing insights and strategies with you in the next chapters. Let's keep moving toward financial freedom together.

Your biggest fan,

Alex

PS: If you know someone who'd benefit from this book, share it with them! Goodwill is contagious, and we all win when we support one another.

Chapter 6: Enhancing Financial Literacy and Mindset

The world of finance often feels like navigating a labyrinth, where each turn introduces unfamiliar terms and concepts that can leave you feeling lost. In this chapter, we aim to demystify the language of finance, empowering you to make informed decisions and take confident strides toward your financial goals. Knowledge is not just power; it's a tool that transforms uncertainty into opportunity.

Understanding financial terminology is crucial for building and managing wealth effectively. Mastering financial language enables you to decipher complex concepts that might otherwise seem intimidating. Terms like "liquidity," which refers to how easily assets can be converted into cash without affecting their market value, help assess financial flexibility in emergencies. Similarly, "asset allocation"—the strategy of distributing investments across various categories like stocks, bonds, and real estate—balances risk and reward based on your goals. "Dividends," portions of a company's earnings distributed to shareholders, often provide a source of passive income. These terms are building blocks for wealth creation, and studies show that increased literacy correlates with greater wealth outcomes (Lusardi & Mitchell, 2013).

Let's simplify more terms: "Amortization" is the gradual repayment of a loan over time, such as a mortgage, where each payment reduces both the principal and interest. "Capital gains" are profits earned from selling an asset like stocks at a price higher than the purchase price. These concepts, applied practically, can help shape your financial strategies.

Misunderstanding terms can lead to costly mistakes. For example, confusing "APR" (Annual Percentage Rate) with "APY" (Annual Percentage Yield) could lead to incorrect calculations of loan costs or investment returns. Similarly, overlooking "credit utilization"—the portion of your credit limit used—can harm your credit score. A personal glossary of financial terms, updated regularly, can provide clarity and empower you to make informed decisions.

6.1 Financial Education: Resources for Continuous Learning

In a world where financial landscapes shift frequently, ongoing education is essential. Staying informed about economic trends equips you to adapt and thrive. Continuous learning is not just about acquiring facts; it's about developing skills to seize opportunities and mitigate risks.

Consider resources like books and online platforms. "Rich Dad Poor Dad" offers foundational insights into wealth-building strategies, while "The Intelligent Investor" delves into value investing. Online platforms like Coursera and Khan Academy provide courses covering budgeting basics to advanced investment strategies. Podcasts and websites simplify complex ideas, offering practical advice tailored to diverse knowledge levels.

Free Resources for Financial Education

For those seeking to deepen their understanding, numerous free resources are available:

- **Government Programs**:
    - *MyMoney.gov* offers guides on budgeting, saving, and planning for retirement.
    - The *Consumer Financial Protection Bureau* provides tools like budgeting worksheets and answers to common financial questions.
- **Nonprofit Organizations**:
    - The *National Endowment for Financial Education (NEFE)* provides unbiased tools and courses on topics like retirement planning and debt management.
    - Local nonprofits like *Operation HOPE* often host workshops and one-on-one coaching sessions.
- **Libraries and Platforms**:
    - Public libraries host free workshops and provide access to personal finance books and eBooks.
    - Khan Academy's personal finance course covers saving, investing, and understanding credit.

Integrating these resources into your routine creates a robust foundation for financial literacy.

Mentorship and Networking: Unlocking Financial Growth

Mentorship and networking are transformative elements of financial education. A mentor offers guidance rooted in real-world experience, while networking connects you with like-minded peers who share your goals and challenges.

How to Find a Mentor

- Use professional networks like LinkedIn to identify experts in your financial niche.
- Attend finance-focused events through platforms like Meetup or Eventbrite.
- Join organizations like SCORE, which provides free mentorship for entrepreneurs.

Building a Financial Community

- Join local investment clubs or personal finance meetups.
- Participate in workshops hosted by community centers or financial institutions.
- Engage in online communities like Reddit's r/personalfinance to exchange tips and ideas.

Through mentorship and networking, you gain confidence, resources, and guidance to navigate your financial journey.

6.2 Mindset Shifts for Financial Empowerment

Shifting your mindset can dramatically impact your financial success.

It's not just about crunching numbers; it's about the thoughts and beliefs that guide your financial decisions. Many people operate from a scarcity mindset, where fear of not having enough drives their actions. This perspective can lead to hoarding resources, avoiding investment opportunities, or even racking up debt out of fear of future shortages. By transitioning to an abundance mindset, you open yourself to possibilities. Abundance thinking encourages you to see the potential in every situation, fostering optimism and creativity in financial planning. Instead of focusing on limitations, you begin to explore how you can grow your resources. Embracing growth-oriented beliefs about money invites a world where you believe in the potential for financial expansion, leading to more strategic and fearless financial decisions.

Developing a success-oriented mindset requires practical strategies. Start with gratitude. Acknowledging the financial abundance you currently have, no matter how small, shifts your focus from what's lacking to what's available. This simple practice can transform your outlook on money, instilling a sense of control and satisfaction. Set affirmations and visualizations for your financial goals. Imagine the life you want to create, and use positive statements to reinforce your vision. Phrases like "I am capable of building wealth" or "I manage my finances wisely" can rewire your thought patterns, encouraging proactive behavior. Regularly visualize your financial goals and the steps needed to achieve them. This mental rehearsal strengthens your commitment and aligns your actions with your aspirations.

Self-awareness plays a crucial role in achieving financial empowerment. Understanding your personal financial tendencies and biases is essential for growth. Start by identifying and challenging any limiting beliefs you may hold about money; these beliefs might stem from childhood experiences or societal messages that shape your views on wealth and success.

Reflect on your past financial decisions. What patterns do you notice? Are there recurring mistakes or avoidance behaviors? By examining these patterns, you can learn from them, paving the way for more informed choices in the future. Self-awareness enables you to recognize what drives your spending habits or investment strategies, helping you make conscious decisions that align with your values.

Consider the story of Daniel, who once felt trapped under the weight of mounting debt, believing it to be an impossible hurdle to overcome. For years, he avoided addressing his financial struggles, seeing them as a source of shame and fear. One day, Daniel decided to take control of his narrative. He began viewing debt not as a permanent burden but as a tool he could manage and eventually overcome. This shift in perspective changed everything.

By adopting an abundance mindset, Daniel identified opportunities to advance his career, boost his income, and create a plan to tackle his financial challenges. He prioritized long-term goals over short-term gratification, such as building an emergency fund and saving for his future. He also committed to investing, recognizing the importance of letting his money grow over time.

Daniel's transformation shows the powerful effect of a mindset shift on financial outcomes. His story proves that when you approach challenges with determination and a growth-oriented perspective, they can evolve into opportunities for lasting empowerment and success.

6.3 Overcoming Financial Anxiety with Knowledge

Financial anxiety is a silent specter hovering over many, impacting decisions and well-being. This anxiety often stems from the unpredictability of income, mounting debts, or the pressure to meet financial obligations. For some, it's the uncertainty of paying bills or the looming specter of student loans. For others, it's the fear of unexpected expenses that could derail their financial plans. This stress doesn't just weigh on your mind; it seeps into your physical health, manifesting as insomnia, headaches, or even more severe ailments. When triggered by financial worries, the body's stress response can lead to heightened blood pressure, muscle tension, and a compromised immune system. Emotionally, it can cause irritability, anxiety, and depression, affecting both personal and professional relationships. Financial anxiety can cloud judgment, leading to decisions driven by fear rather than reason, perpetuating a cycle of stress and financial instability. This stress, if left unchecked, can lead to avoidance behaviors, such as ignoring bills or avoiding financial discussions, which only exacerbate the problem.

Knowledge is a powerful antidote to financial anxiety. By educating yourself on personal finance, you can replace fear with clarity and confidence. Tackling intimidating topics head-on—whether it's understanding interest rates, investment strategies, or mastering budgeting techniques—allows you to demystify these areas and take control of your financial future. Here's how you can explore these topics in greater depth:

Choose Your Starting Point

Focus on the financial topics that feel most intimidating or urgent for you.

- Interest Rates: Learn how interest rates affect loans, credit cards, and savings accounts. Tools like Bankrate or free online calculators can help you compare rates and understand their impact on your financial decisions.

- Budgeting Techniques: Explore methods like the 50/30/20 rule or zero-based budgeting. Apps like YNAB (You Need A Budget) or Mint provide hands-on learning tools to create and manage your budget effectively.
- Investment Strategies: Begin with the basics, such as understanding stocks, bonds, and ETFs. Platforms like Investopedia offer beginner-friendly guides and glossaries to break down complex concepts.

Leverage Books and Online Courses

Books and courses provide structured learning tailored to different levels of expertise:

- Books:
    - The Total Money Makeover by Dave Ramsey for foundational budgeting and debt strategies.
    - The Simple Path to Wealth by JL Collins for straightforward investment advice.
    - Your Money or Your Life by Vicki Robin for a mindset shift on money and life balance.
- Online Courses:
    - Free options on Coursera and Khan Academy cover personal finance basics.
    - Affordable classes on Udemy and Skillshare focus on niche topics like investing or financial independence.

Attend Workshops and Seminars

- Look for local workshops hosted by community centers, libraries, or financial institutions. These often cover practical topics such as tax planning, retirement strategies, or managing debt.

- Check online for webinars or virtual summits, like those offered by organizations such as FinCon or NerdWallet, to access expert advice from the comfort of home.

Seek Professional Advice

Working with a financial advisor or counselor can provide tailored strategies and clarity:

- Financial Advisors: Professionals certified in personal finance (CFP) can help you craft a comprehensive plan. Seek recommendations through NAPFA (National Association of Personal Financial Advisors) or use platforms like SmartAsset to find vetted advisors.
- Credit Counselors: Nonprofit organizations like the National Foundation for Credit Counseling (NFCC) offer free or low-cost services to help manage debt and improve financial literacy.

Join Communities and Forums

Engage with others who are learning and discussing personal finance:

- Online Communities: Platforms like Reddit's r/personalfinance or Facebook groups focused on money management foster peer-to-peer learning and encouragement.
- Local Groups: Join investment clubs or personal finance meetups to exchange ideas and strategies with others in your area.

Create a Personal Action Plan

- Break down intimidating topics into manageable steps. For example:
    - If interest rates overwhelm you, start by understanding how they work, then review the rates on your loans or credit cards.
    - If budgeting feels complicated, begin with one month of tracking expenses using a simple tool like Excel or an app.
- Set realistic goals for your learning journey, such as completing one book or attending a workshop within a specific timeframe.

Practice What You Learn

Knowledge becomes powerful when put into action. Start small:

- Open a savings account with a competitive interest rate.
- Create a simple monthly budget based on your current spending habits.
- Invest a modest amount in a low-cost index fund to understand how investing works firsthand.

You can transform financial anxiety into confidence by exploring these resources and taking actionable steps. The more you learn, the more empowered you'll feel to make informed decisions that align with your goals. Remember, financial literacy is a journey, not a destination—every step forward is progress.

In addition to education, mindfulness and relaxation techniques can be powerful tools for alleviating financial stress and fostering a clearer perspective. Practices like mindful breathing exercises allow you to anchor yourself in the present moment, reducing the immediate stress response and creating mental space to approach financial challenges with a calmer mindset. Simply dedicating a few minutes each day to focusing on your breath—perhaps using a simple counting method or a guided app—can establish a foundation of tranquility.

Guided meditations, particularly those designed to address financial clarity, are another effective way to cultivate a balanced mindset. These meditations often include visualization exercises that help you imagine achieving your financial goals and outline actionable steps to get there, creating a sense of empowerment and control. Resources like the Calm app, Insight Timer, and Headspace offer a variety of guided meditations, including those tailored to managing stress and fostering financial confidence.

For deeper relaxation, practices like progressive muscle relaxation or yoga can be instrumental. By intentionally releasing physical tension and calming the nervous system, these techniques can further enhance your ability to make rational, thoughtful decisions about your finances. Incorporating mindfulness into your daily routine helps you build emotional resilience, ensuring that financial decisions are guided by logic and long-term goals rather than immediate stress or anxiety. Through these practices, you reduce financial strain and gain clarity and confidence in managing your financial journey.

Consider Mia, a young professional weighed down by student loans that seemed to dominate her thoughts and limit her opportunities. Each month, the stress of her loan payments overshadowed her daily life, making her feel stuck in a financial rut. Determined to take control, Mia began researching debt management strategies and sought guidance from a financial counselor. Together, they crafted a repayment plan tailored to her budget, incorporating strategies like consolidating her loans and prioritizing higher-interest debts. Over time, as her debt decreased, so did her anxiety. With a clearer mind and a sustainable plan, Mia found herself able to focus on her career and other life goals, feeling empowered by her progress.

In contrast, Richard, a retiree, spent years feeling uneasy about whether his savings would last through retirement. The uncertainty cast a shadow over his ability to enjoy his hard-earned free time. Seeking clarity, Richard attended financial workshops and scheduled meetings with advisors who specialized in retirement planning. Together, they designed a sustainable income plan that balanced his investments and withdrawals. With a clear understanding of his finances and a reliable strategy in place, Richard finally felt at ease. He began to embrace his retirement, free from the financial fears that had once weighed heavily on him.

Mia and Richard's experiences demonstrate the transformative power of combining education with mindful planning. They overcame their financial anxieties by taking deliberate steps to learn and manage stress, gaining confidence and stability. Their stories prove that knowledge, guidance, and a proactive approach make it possible to navigate even the most complex financial challenges and achieve lasting well-being.

6.4 The Role of Emotions in Financial Decisions

In the world of personal finance, emotions play a powerful and often underestimated role. They quietly shape decisions, sometimes leading us astray from logic and long-term goals. Fear and greed, for example, are particularly influential when it comes to investments. Fear might prevent you from taking calculated risks, leaving your money stagnant and missing opportunities for growth. Conversely, greed can tempt you into impulsive choices, such as chasing risky investments for quick profits without fully considering potential losses. This emotional push and pull can create a cycle of reactive decision-making, where choices are driven by the moment rather than by strategy.

Happiness and stress also leave their mark on financial behavior. Take Clara, for instance, a young professional who often indulged in shopping sprees after a tough week at work. The thrill of buying something new temporarily lifted her mood, but over time, these unplanned expenses began to undermine her ability to save for a home. Clara's story is not uncommon—emotions like satisfaction and frustration frequently influence spending, often leading to short-term gratification at the expense of long-term stability.

Recognizing Emotional Triggers

Learning to identify and understand emotional triggers is a vital step in gaining control over your financial decisions. For instance, Clara began noticing that her stress-related shopping habits followed particularly challenging days at work. She realized that she wasn't addressing the root cause of her stress, which led her to explore healthier coping mechanisms, such as exercising or journaling, instead of reaching for her credit card. Recognizing these patterns gave her the power to interrupt them and make more deliberate choices.

Javier, a middle-aged investor, experienced a different set of triggers. He was anxious during market downturns and tempted to sell off investments at a loss to avoid further decline. After reflecting on his emotions, Javier realized his fear stemmed from uncertainty about how markets recover. He sought education on market cycles and began consulting a trusted financial advisor. Over time, his confidence grew, and he became less reactive to short-term fluctuations, focusing instead on his long-term strategy.

Reflecting on your emotions can help you see how they influence your actions. Do you overspend when you feel bored, stressed, or overwhelmed? Do you avoid making investment decisions because you fear losing money? Tracking these patterns is key to understanding how emotions shape your financial behaviors.

Managing Emotional Influences

Building emotional intelligence in financial matters is essential for mitigating these emotional effects. This involves cultivating self-awareness and developing tools to manage your responses effectively. One practical approach is to practice delayed gratification. When tempted to make an impulsive purchase, pause and give yourself a cooling-off period. For example, Clara started implementing a 48-hour rule before making any non-essential purchases. This simple practice helped her evaluate whether the expense aligned with her financial goals or was simply a fleeting desire.

Another effective strategy is to maintain a financial emotions journal. Write down your thoughts and feelings around financial decisions—what triggered them, how you reacted, and the outcomes. Over time, this practice helps uncover patterns and recurring triggers. Clara's journaling revealed that her shopping habits were often a response to work stress, while Javier identified his market-related anxiety through similar reflection.

Mindfulness techniques can also help you manage financial stress. Practices like deep breathing or guided meditations focused on clarity and control allow you to create mental space and approach decisions with a calm mindset. Resources like the Calm app or Insight Timer offer guided meditations specifically designed to address financial anxiety and promote focus.

Transformative Stories of Emotional Mastery

Real-life examples demonstrate the transformative power of mastering emotional triggers. Consider Javier's journey: By recognizing his fear of market downturns and seeking education, he preserved his investments and grew more confident in his financial strategies. Similarly, Clara's shift from emotional spending to mindful saving enabled her to put money aside for her first home—an achievement she had long considered out of reach.

Then there's the story of the Patel family, who struggled with emotional spending tied to their desire to keep up appearances. By starting weekly family meetings to discuss financial priorities, they shifted their focus from immediate wants to shared values like saving for their children's education. This open communication fostered collaboration and reduced the stress of financial misalignment.

Turning Emotional Awareness Into Empowerment

You can confidently make financial decisions by learning to recognize emotional triggers and their effects. Building self-awareness through reflection and mindfulness, alongside practical tools like journaling and delayed gratification, creates a foundation for rational and intentional choices. Stories like those of Clara, Javier, and the Patel family remind us that emotions don't have to control our finances. Instead, when approached with awareness and thoughtful strategies, they can serve as guideposts, leading to growth, stability, and long-term empowerment.

6.5 Building a Community of Financial Support

Navigating personal finance challenges alone can feel overwhelming, but building a financial support network can provide encouragement and accountability. Connecting with like-minded individuals offers shared experiences that enhance resilience and make financial goals more attainable. Imagine having partners who check in, offer support, and help you stay focused.

A financial community also provides valuable emotional support during setbacks, making challenges feel more manageable. Local resources such as community centers, libraries, and universities often host financial workshops where you can gain skills and meet others. Websites like Meetup and Eventbrite offer opportunities to find local investment clubs or personal finance meetups.

Organizations like SCORE and small business development centers provide mentoring and workshops that are beneficial for entrepreneurs. Engaging in financial challenges, such as savings sprints, fosters camaraderie and shared purpose.

Social media platforms like Twitter, LinkedIn, and Facebook have vibrant personal finance communities where you can connect with influencers and peers. These communities create opportunities for learning and growth. By seeking out these connections, you turn financial challenges into collaborative opportunities, making your journey toward your financial goals more rewarding and manageable.

Chapter 7: Adapting to Life Changes and Transitions

Life is a series of transitions, each bringing its own set of financial challenges and opportunities. Whether you're stepping into a new career, purchasing your first home, or preparing for retirement, these milestones require thoughtful financial planning. Imagine standing at the edge of a forest, about to embark on a journey through unfamiliar terrain. Each step represents a decision, a move forward into the unknown. The path is not always clear, but with preparation and foresight, you can navigate these transitions confidently. Let's explore how you can plan for major life events, ensuring that your financial footing remains secure even as the landscape shifts.

7.1 Financial Planning for Major Life Events

Major life events can significantly impact your financial landscape, often requiring adjustments to existing plans. Buying a home, for instance, is not just about the excitement of new beginnings. It brings with it increased expenses, from the down payment and closing costs to ongoing maintenance and property taxes. These costs can stretch your budget, necessitating careful planning to avoid financial strain. A career change, whether by choice or necessity, also demands attention to your finances. It may mean adjusting your budget to accommodate a new salary or managing a period of reduced income during the transition. Similarly, retirement, while a time of relaxation and enjoyment, requires a solid financial plan to ensure that your savings can sustain your lifestyle. Each of these events is a financial milestone that requires careful consideration and strategic planning.

Proactive planning is key to managing these transitions smoothly. Begin by creating a timeline for anticipated expenses. This timeline acts as a roadmap, guiding you through the financial demands of each stage. For example, if buying a home is on the horizon, start by setting financial milestones aligned with that goal. Determine how much you need to save for a down payment, and create a monthly savings plan to reach that target. Similarly, if you're considering a career change, outline the financial implications and prepare for potential income fluctuations. This might involve building a savings cushion to cover expenses during the transition period. Setting clear financial milestones helps you stay focused and motivated, ensuring that you're prepared for whatever life throws your way.

Emergency preparedness is another crucial element of financial planning during life transitions. Establishing a contingency fund for unforeseen expenses provides a safety net, helping you weather unexpected challenges without derailing your financial plans. This fund should cover at least three to six months of living expenses, offering peace of mind and stability. Periodic assessments of your emergency fund are essential, ensuring that it remains adequate as your financial situation evolves. Life is unpredictable, and having a robust emergency fund allows you to face unexpected events with confidence, whether it's a medical emergency, a sudden job loss, or an unforeseen home repair.

Interactive Element: Crafting Your Timeline

1. **Identify Major Life Events**: List events such as buying a home, changing careers, or retirement that you anticipate in the near future.

2. **Set Financial Milestones**: For each event, determine key financial goals, such as saving for a down payment or building a retirement fund.

3. **Create a Timeline**: Lay out a schedule for achieving these milestones, with monthly or quarterly checkpoints to track progress.

4. **Review and Adjust**: Regularly assess your timeline, making adjustments as needed to stay on track.

Real-life examples illustrate the power of strategic financial planning. Consider a couple who dreamed of owning their home. Through disciplined saving and careful budgeting, they gradually amassed the funds needed for a down payment. By setting clear milestones and sticking to their timeline, they turned their dream into reality. Another example is a retiree who transitioned smoothly into retirement. Through years of diligent planning, they built a nest egg that allowed them to enjoy their golden years without financial worry. These stories show that with the right preparation, you can navigate life's transitions with confidence and ease.

7.2 Transitioning to Self-Employment: Financial Considerations

Stepping into self-employment is like trading a paved road for an unmarked trail. The freedom to be your own boss and set your own schedule is undeniably enticing, but it comes with a unique set of financial challenges. Irregular income flows can make it difficult to predict cash availability, with one month bringing abundance and the next sparking uncertainty. Expenses, too, can fluctuate widely, encompassing costs like equipment, supplies, and marketing. Successfully managing these variables requires sharp financial planning and discipline.

Understanding Taxes in Self-Employment

One of the most complex aspects of self-employment is managing taxes. Unlike traditional employees whose taxes are withheld by their employers, self-employed individuals must calculate and pay taxes independently. This includes self-employment taxes, which cover Social Security and Medicare contributions, often requiring quarterly payments. Failing to account for these taxes can lead to financial strain, making early preparation crucial.

Meticulous record-keeping is key to navigating tax obligations. Maintain detailed records of your income and expenses to ensure accurate reporting and maximize deductions. For instance:

- **Home Office Deduction**: If you use a portion of your home exclusively for business, you may deduct related expenses.

- **Travel and Meals**: Business-related travel expenses, including lodging and meals, can often be deducted.

- **Equipment Purchases**: Items necessary for your business, such as computers, software, or tools, may qualify for deductions.

Tax planning isn't just about meeting obligations; it's an opportunity to retain more of your hard-earned income through strategic deductions. Consulting a tax professional is vital to ensure compliance and to fully understand what you can deduct.

Essential Disclaimer

This book is intended to provide general information on financial management for self-employment. It should not be construed as legal or tax advice. Always seek guidance from a certified tax professional or financial advisor to address your specific circumstances and ensure compliance with tax laws.

Resources for Tax Education

Understanding self-employment taxes requires proactive learning. Here are some resources to help:

- **IRS Small Business and Self-Employed Tax Center**: A comprehensive guide to federal tax obligations for self-employed individuals.

- **Local Small Business Development Centers (SBDCs)**: Many SBDCs offer free or low-cost workshops on taxes and financial management.

- **Books**: Titles like *Taxes for Small Businesses for Dummies* by Eric Tyson provide accessible explanations of self-employment tax responsibilities.

- **Online Courses**: Platforms like Coursera and Udemy offer tax-specific courses tailored to freelancers and entrepreneurs.

- **Professional Associations**: Organizations like the National Association for the Self-Employed (NASE) provide tools and educational resources for managing taxes and deductions.

Establishing Financial Stability

As we have already established in our personal lives, the same is true for our self-employment journey: a realistic budget is the cornerstone of financial security in self-employment. Start by identifying your fixed and variable expenses, covering essentials like rent, utilities, and groceries. From there, factor in your business needs, such as advertising, software subscriptions, or travel expenses. Allocating funds to these areas ensures you stay within your means while maintaining the resources necessary for growth.

Equally important is building a cash reserve for weather-lean periods. As with our personal finances, aim to save enough to cover three to six months of living expenses, creating a financial buffer that alleviates stress and allows you to focus on expanding your business. Automating savings or designating a portion of high-income months to your reserve can make this process easier.

The Value of Professional Advice

Navigating self-employment finances is significantly easier with the guidance of a professional. A certified financial advisor or accountant can help you:

- Optimize your tax strategy by identifying deductions and credits.
- Establish systems for tracking income and expenses efficiently.
- Create a financial plan that supports both personal and business goals.

Their expertise simplifies tax season and empowers you to maximize your financial potential.

Consider the journey of Michelle, a freelance graphic designer who transitioned from a stable corporate job to the unpredictable world of self-employment. Initially, she felt overwhelmed by fluctuating income and tax obligations. She gained clarity and confidence by seeking advice from an accountant and setting up a detailed tracking system for her finances. This framework allowed her to focus on client work, build her reputation, and eventually achieve financial stability.

Similarly, Raj, a self-employed consultant, faced challenges balancing personal and business expenses. He established clear financial goals, diligently saved during high-income months, and created a cash reserve. With the help of a tax professional, Raj streamlined his quarterly tax payments and maximized deductions, allowing him to reinvest in his business and achieve steady growth.

Your Path Forward

Self-employment offers unmatched freedom but requires proactive financial management to thrive. Understanding taxes, leveraging resources, and seeking professional guidance can transform financial challenges into opportunities. With a strategic approach, the unmarked trail of self-employment becomes a path to success, resilience, and growth.

7.3 Navigating Marriage, Divorce, and Family Dynamics

Marriage and divorce are two sides of a coin, each carrying profound implications for personal finances. When two lives intertwine in marriage, so do their finances. The decision to combine finances and establish joint accounts often marks a new chapter of shared financial responsibility. This can simplify expenses and build a collective savings goal, yet it also requires open communication and mutual understanding. *It's essential to discuss financial habits, set joint goals, and agree on a budgeting strategy that respects both partners' perspectives.* This can prevent misunderstandings and foster a collaborative approach to managing shared resources. However, the financial landscape shifts dramatically when a marriage ends in divorce. Assets and liabilities must be divided, often necessitating a reevaluation of one's financial footing. Legal fees, alimony, and child support can further complicate the picture, requiring a strategic reassessment of budget and resources. Divorce can feel like a financial earthquake, shaking the foundation you've built. Yet, with careful planning and support, it's possible to rebuild and regain stability.

Open financial communication is vital during both marriage and divorce. Establishing clear financial goals as a couple creates a roadmap for shared aspirations, from buying a home to saving for retirement or planning vacations. These goals provide a mutual focus, aligning your financial decisions with your shared values. They offer a framework within which to negotiate spending, saving, and investing. During a separation, creating a financial agreement can ease the transition. This agreement outlines the division of assets and liabilities, guiding the process with clarity and fairness. It serves as a reference point during negotiations, reducing the potential for conflict. Setting these parameters early can prevent the emotional toll that financial disagreements often bring, allowing both parties to move forward with a sense of security and understanding.

Seeking professional advice during these times can be a game-changer. A financial planner can offer guidance on how to merge finances effectively, helping to create a comprehensive plan that accounts for both individual and joint goals. They provide an objective perspective, identifying potential pitfalls and opportunities. During a divorce, working with a mediator or attorney becomes crucial. These professionals help navigate the legal complexities, ensuring that asset division and support agreements are equitable and sustainable. They can offer insights into tax implications, retirement accounts, and the long-term impact of financial decisions. With their support, you can make informed choices that protect your financial future, even as the emotional landscape shifts.

Consider the narrative of a couple who successfully aligned their financial vision. They began with separate accounts but gradually integrated their finances, setting joint goals for travel and home ownership. Through regular discussions and adjustments, they maintained flexibility, adapting their plan as circumstances changed. This approach strengthened their partnership, allowing them to thrive financially and personally. Now consider the story of a divorcee rebuilding financial independence. After the initial upheaval, they focused on creating a new budget that reflected their changed circumstances. By setting realistic goals and seeking professional advice, they rebuilt their financial foundation. This process restored confidence and provided the freedom to pursue new opportunities. Their journey highlights the resilience and adaptability required to navigate the financial complexities of marriage and divorce.

7.4 Balancing Finances in Single-Income Households

Living in a single-income household can feel like walking a financial tightrope. The pressure to manage all expenses with one paycheck often looms large, creating a unique set of challenges. When your income is limited, every dollar must stretch further. This means carefully managing expenses, ensuring essentials like rent, utilities, and groceries are covered while also trying to set aside money for savings and unexpected costs. Balancing these demands requires careful planning and discipline, as even a minor financial hiccup can have significant repercussions. For many, the idea of building savings under these constraints seems daunting, yet it remains a crucial component of financial security. The challenge lies in finding ways to save without sacrificing the basics, a task that demands creativity and resilience.

To maintain stability in a single-income household, it is essential to prioritize expenses. Start by distinguishing between needs and wants. This doesn't mean living a life devoid of enjoyment but rather focusing on what is truly necessary for your family's well-being. Consider cutting non-essential expenses, such as dining out or subscription services, to free up funds for more pressing needs. Exploring additional income opportunities can also bolster your financial standing. This might involve taking on a side hustle or part-time job that fits your schedule. Whether it's freelance writing, crafting products to sell online, or offering tutoring services, these additional income streams can provide a valuable financial cushion. They contribute not only to your day-to-day living expenses but also to building a safety net for the future.

Community support can be a lifeline for single-income households. Many organizations and programs are designed to assist individuals and families facing financial hardships. Local food banks, for instance, offer essential groceries, easing the burden on your budget. Assistance programs can provide support with utility bills or childcare costs, allowing you to allocate resources more effectively.

These community resources are there to help, and utilizing them can significantly ease financial pressure. Seeking support is not a sign of weakness; it's a practical step toward ensuring your family's well-being. Engaging with community programs can also connect you with others in similar situations, offering a network of support and shared experiences.

Real-life stories offer inspiration and proof that thriving on a single income is possible. Take the example of a single parent balancing work and family. With careful budgeting and utilizing community resources, they successfully manage household expenses while providing for their children. This parent embraces the challenge of finding ways to enrich their family's life without overspending. Similarly, consider a couple succeeding on one salary. They prioritize their spending, focusing on what matters most to them, such as saving for their children's education and planning for the future. This couple takes advantage of side hustles, turning hobbies into additional income sources that supplement their primary earnings. These stories highlight the power of strategic planning and community support in overcoming the challenges of a single-income household.

7.5 Preparing for Parenthood: Financial Readiness

Welcoming a child into your family is a momentous occasion, one filled with joy and profound change. Yet, the arrival of a little one also brings significant financial implications that require careful consideration. Parenthood transforms your household budget, as there are new expenses to accommodate—diapers, childcare, and education, to name a few. These costs accumulate quickly, pressing on your monthly budget and long-term financial plans. Childcare alone can become a substantial expense, often rivaling rent or mortgage payments. Education, too, becomes a priority, whether you're planning for preschool or pondering future college costs. This shift calls for a reevaluation of lifestyle and spending habits, making room for the needs of a growing family.

To prepare financially for this new chapter, consider setting up a savings plan specifically for child-related expenses. Start by estimating the cost of essentials like diapers, clothing, and baby gear, then factor in potential childcare costs. Establishing a dedicated savings account can help manage these expenses, ensuring you're ready when they arise. Healthcare and insurance options also deserve attention. Reviewing your health insurance plan to understand coverage for prenatal care, delivery, and pediatric visits is crucial. Adjusting your insurance to fit your growing family's needs can prevent unexpected medical bills from straining your finances. Additionally, consider life insurance policies that secure your family's financial future, providing peace of mind in case of unforeseen circumstances.

Long-term planning is equally vital when preparing for parenthood. Think about the future expenses your child may incur, including education and extracurricular activities. Starting a college fund early can alleviate the financial burden when the time comes. Options like a 529 savings plan offer tax advantages and flexibility, allowing you to save systematically over the years. Even small contributions can grow significantly over time, easing the financial pressure of higher education. Planning for extracurricular activities—sports, music lessons, or camps—ensures that your child can explore their interests without financial constraints. These plans not only secure your child's future but also allow you to manage your finances with foresight and confidence.

Consider the story of a couple who took proactive steps to ensure financial readiness for their child's future. They began by creating a detailed budget that accounted for both immediate and future expenses. By setting aside a portion of their income each month, they built a substantial college fund before their child even started school. This financial foresight allowed them to focus on enjoying their family time without constant financial worry. Similarly, a single parent diligently managed early childhood costs by prioritizing spending and seeking community resources. By accessing local programs and support networks, they could provide for their child's needs without compromising their financial stability. These examples illustrate the power of strategic planning and resourcefulness in preparing for parenthood.

Scenario: Financial Planning for a Single-Income Household

Consider the story of Sarah and James, who recently welcomed their first child. Sarah decided to stay home to care for their baby, transitioning the family to James's single income of $75,000 annually. The change in income required careful financial planning and awareness of tax implications.

1. **Tax Filing Status and Withholding Adjustments:** They updated their filing status to "Married Filing Jointly" and revised James's W-4 to ensure accurate withholding, reflecting the new child as a dependent.

2. **Child Tax Credit and Dependent Care Benefits:** They became eligible for the Child Tax

Credit, which reduced their tax liability by $2,000. Additionally, James's employer offered a Dependent Care Flexible Spending Account, enabling pre-tax contributions toward childcare expenses.

3. **Budget Adjustments:** The couple reevaluated their household budget to accommodate the single income. They focused on reducing discretionary spending, prioritizing savings, and building an emergency fund to cover three months of expenses.

4. **Retirement Planning:** Despite the income shift, they maintained contributions to James's 401(k) to leverage employer matching. Sarah began contributing to a spousal IRA, taking advantage of the tax benefits for non-working spouses.

5. **Professional Advice:** They consulted a local tax preparer who ensured they maximized available deductions and credits. The preparer also advised them on future tax-saving strategies, such as opening a 529 Plan for their child's education.

By planning carefully, Sarah and James adjusted to their new financial reality, minimizing the transition's impact while securing their financial future.

7.6 Embracing Change: Financial Resilience Amidst Transitions

Life is full of changes, and financial resilience is your greatest asset in navigating the uncertainties they bring. It's the ability to adapt and stay grounded when circumstances shift, whether due to market fluctuations or personal challenges. Resilience empowers you to reassess your financial goals, adjust your strategies, and explore new opportunities without losing sight of what matters most.

Building resilience requires both mindset and action. Regularly reviewing your financial plans ensures they evolve with your circumstances while cultivating diverse income streams provides stability in uncertain times. Embracing change with flexibility allows you to turn challenges into opportunities, unlocking potential where others see obstacles.

Resilience is not just a response to adversity—it's a skill that strengthens over time. As you navigate life's transitions, let it guide you toward stability, growth, and discovery. With a resilient approach, you're not just weathering change; you're thriving through it, confident in your ability to shape the future on your terms.

Chapter 8 Achieving Long-Term Financial Goals

Picture planning your financial future as setting the coordinates for a long journey across uncharted waters. Without a clear destination, you risk drifting aimlessly, swayed by life's unforeseen currents. Though shaped by income and expenses, your financial path begins with envisioning where you wish to go. Long-term financial planning isn't just about numbers; it's about aligning your financial journey with your core values and life aspirations. This alignment creates a roadmap that guides your decisions, ensuring each step on your path brings you closer to your dreams. Whether you aspire to retire comfortably, buy a home, or achieve financial independence, having a clear vision is crucial. It's about defining what success looks like to you and creating a plan that reflects your values. This clarity not only helps you prioritize your financial goals but also keeps you focused on what truly matters, even amidst life's distractions.

To navigate this complex landscape, it's helpful to adopt a structured approach to goal setting. A method we have relied on already is the SMART criteria (Specific, Measurable, Achievable, Realistic, and Time-bound goals). This framework transforms vague ambitions into actionable plans. For example, instead of saying, "I want to save for retirement," a SMART goal would be, "I will contribute $100 monthly to my retirement fund for the next 10 years" (FinMasters, n.d.). This specificity provides clarity, while measurability allows you to track progress. Ensuring your goals are achievable and realistic keeps them within reach, avoiding discouragement. Setting a time-bound deadline instills a sense of urgency and accountability, propelling you toward your objectives with purpose and determination (Khan Academy, n.d.). Incorporating your life aspirations into these goals ensures that your financial plan resonates with your values, making the journey toward achieving them more meaningful and rewarding.

Visualization breathes life into the SMART framework, turning abstract goals into vivid mental images. Visualization helps you connect emotionally to your goals, making them more motivating and tangible. For instance, if your SMART goal is to save $20,000 for a down payment on a house within three years, imagine the moment you hold the keys to your new home. Picture walking through the front door, decorating the living room, or hosting a housewarming party. These mental images reinforce your commitment, creating a tangible sense of purpose that keeps you inspired throughout the journey.

Take the Dawson family. Determined to achieve financial independence, they began by setting clear, actionable goals, such as eliminating debt and building a substantial emergency fund. To stay motivated, they aligned these goals with their desire for security and freedom, even when faced with setbacks. Visualization helped them picture each milestone—paying off a credit card, watching their emergency fund grow, and finally reaching their ultimate goal of financial independence. Through dedication and purpose-driven planning, they achieved their dreams, empowered by a vision that aligned with their values.

Similarly, a young professional might set a SMART goal to retire early. They could outline a plan involving disciplined savings and strategic investments. Visualization could play a crucial role by keeping their focus sharp—imagining a future filled with travel, creative pursuits, or time spent with loved ones. By combining SMART goal setting with visualization, they remain connected to the bigger picture, finding the motivation to push forward despite challenges.

Here's how to integrate SMART goals with visualization techniques for maximum impact:

1. **Define Your Goal and Create a Visual Anchor**: Write down your SMART goal with all its details, such as "I will save $500 per month to reach $6,000 for an emergency fund within 12 months." Pair this goal with a visual representation like a vision board featuring images of security or a graph tracking your monthly savings.

2. **Visualize the Steps, Not Just the Destination**: Imagine the smaller steps you'll take to achieve your goal, such as setting aside savings each week or fine-tuning your budget. These incremental visuals reinforce the actionable aspects of your SMART goal.

3. **Tie Visualization to Measurable Milestones**: Break your goal into smaller milestones, such as saving $5,000 out of a $10,000 target. Visualize the celebrations you'll have at each stage, whether it's a small reward or simply reflecting on your progress.

4. **Engage Your Emotions**: Visualization is most effective when it connects emotionally. Imagine the relief, pride, or joy you'll feel when your goal is achieved. Use these emotions to reinforce your determination and keep you focused on your goals.

5. **Revisit and Adjust**: Life evolves, and so should your goals and visualizations. Regularly revisiting and updating your mental imagery ensures that it remains relevant and inspiring.

By blending the clarity of SMART goals with the motivational power of visualization, you create a strategy for achieving financial dreams that is both structured and emotionally engaging. This approach ensures your goals are deeply rooted in your personal aspirations, keeping you inspired and empowered every step of the way.

8.1 Avoiding Lifestyle Inflation: Staying on Track

Lifestyle inflation is like a quiet thief that gradually erodes financial progress. As income rises, it's tempting to elevate spending to match, often without realizing it. Known as lifestyle creep, this subtle shift can lead to living beyond one's means despite a higher paycheck. Upgrading to a larger home, dining at expensive restaurants, or purchasing the latest gadgets may feel justified, but these decisions can significantly diminish savings and investments. Over time, this can create a cycle where each raise or bonus is consumed by new expenses, leaving little to show for increased earnings. *Higher income may not translate into greater financial security or wealth without intentional planning.*

To combat lifestyle inflation, intentional spending is key. Beyond automating transfers to savings or investment accounts, there are several realistic ways to manage income growth effectively while enjoying the present:

Redirecting raises or bonuses toward specific goals can be transformative. For instance, use windfalls to pay down high-interest debt, boost an emergency fund, or contribute to a retirement account. These deliberate choices prevent lifestyle creep and accelerate progress toward financial stability. Creating targeted savings accounts—such as one for a future vacation or home improvement project—helps allocate discretionary funds without derailing long-term goals.

Adopting a delayed gratification approach to major purchases can also curb lifestyle inflation. Instead of immediately upgrading to a more expensive car or electronic device, take time to assess whether the purchase aligns with your priorities. This pause often reveals whether the item truly enhances your life or merely satisfies a fleeting desire.

Another strategy involves practicing mindful spending. Rather than mindlessly increasing expenses, evaluate your current lifestyle and consider which changes would genuinely add value. For example, if dining out is an occasional treat, intentionally maintaining that frequency can prevent costs from spiraling while preserving enjoyment.

Living below one's means remains one of the most effective tools for financial success. It offers a sense of stability and peace of mind, ensuring that fluctuations in income or unexpected expenses won't derail financial plans. A modest lifestyle allows for greater flexibility to pursue goals like travel, education, or early retirement. It also fosters gratitude by shifting the focus from acquiring material possessions to cherishing experiences and relationships. This approach often leads to a more fulfilling and balanced life, guided by personal values rather than societal pressures.

Consider Ava, a marketing executive who resisted the urge to inflate her lifestyle after receiving a significant promotion. Instead of moving to a luxury apartment, she chose to stay in her modest rental while investing the difference in index funds. Over the years, her growing portfolio provided her with financial independence, enabling her to pursue a creative passion without monetary concerns. Similarly, James and Emily, a couple in their 30s, decided to continue driving their reliable, older vehicles despite substantial pay raises. They built a strong financial foundation by redirecting those potential car payments toward their children's education fund and retirement savings while still enjoying meaningful experiences like family camping trips.

These stories underscore the importance of resisting lifestyle inflation. By making intentional choices and focusing on long-term priorities, you can transform increased income into lasting financial success, ensuring that each step forward truly enhances your life.

8.2 Tracking Progress and Celebrating Milestones: Staying Motivated on Your Financial Journey

Keeping track of your financial progress is like steering a ship toward your goals; small corrections along the way ensure you stay on course. Monitoring your financial journey is not just about identifying areas for improvement but also about celebrating the wins that motivate you to keep going. Combining these practices creates a powerful feedback loop that fosters accountability, satisfaction, and long-term success.

Tracking Progress: Tools for Financial Clarity

Regularly assessing your financial standing allows you to identify trends, adjust strategies, and stay aligned with your long-term objectives. A monthly financial review is a practical way to maintain oversight without feeling overwhelmed. Dedicate a consistent time each month to gathering financial statements, reviewing expenses, and comparing your progress against your goals.

Here's a simple framework for an effective financial review:

1. **Update Your Budget and Tracking Tools:** Record income, expenses, and savings in a spreadsheet or app.

2. **Analyze Spending Patterns:** Look for areas where spending exceeded expectations or where savings could be increased.

3. **Compare Against Goals:** Determine how close you are to reaching milestones like paying off debt, growing savings, or hitting investment targets.

4. **Adjust Plans as Needed:** Shift budgets or reallocate resources to stay aligned with your priorities.

5. **Visualize Progress:** Use charts or graphs to see how far you've come, which can make your accomplishments more tangible.

This routine helps you build confidence in your ability to manage finances effectively, providing clarity and direction as you navigate your financial journey.

The Power of Celebrating Milestones

Acknowledging your financial achievements, no matter how small, is crucial for maintaining motivation. Celebrations not only reinforce the habits that led to success but also provide an emotional reward that makes the journey more enjoyable. Each milestone—whether it's saving your first $1,000, paying off a credit card, or completing a major financial goal—deserves recognition.

Ways to Celebrate:

- Treat yourself to a modest reward, like a special meal or a day out with loved ones.
- Host a small gathering to share your achievements with family or friends who have supported you.
- Invest in something meaningful, such as a course or tool that supports your next financial goal.

For example, Sarah, a young professional, celebrated paying off her student loans with a weekend getaway—a symbolic reward for years of diligence. Similarly, the Garcias, a family of four, hosted a dinner party in their newly renovated kitchen after saving for years to make it happen. These celebrations weren't just moments of joy; they were affirmations of hard work and commitment.

Combining Tracking and Celebrating

The act of measuring progress and celebrating milestones works best when integrated into a cohesive financial strategy. Each time you review your finances, identify areas where you've excelled and take a moment to acknowledge those achievements. For instance:

- Completing a monthly financial review might reveal that you've stayed under budget for three consecutive months—an excellent reason to celebrate with a small treat.
- Reaching a savings goal could coincide with planning your next financial target, keeping the momentum alive.

This integrated approach ensures that progress and achievements are not just numbers on a page but meaningful markers of your journey. It turns financial management into a source of pride and joy, empowering you to stay the course and reach even greater heights. By combining the practicality of tracking with the positivity of celebrating, you create a balanced, fulfilling approach to financial growth.

8.3 Leveraging Income Flexibility for Financial Growth

Embracing the potential of variable income can turn financial uncertainty into opportunities for growth. Fluctuating earnings offer flexibility, enabling you to adapt quickly to market changes and explore diverse investment avenues. This adaptability allows for strategic resource allocation and the ability to invest in promising startups or high-growth ventures that align with your risk appetite.

To maximize income flexibility, diversify your investments across stocks, bonds, real estate, and venture capital. Spreading risk can mitigate losses and enhance the chances of significant returns. Investing extra income in rapidly expanding sectors can be particularly rewarding, but thorough research and risk assessment are essential. Consult financial experts to guide your choices.

A flexible financial approach leads to greater resilience amid economic fluctuations. It allows for quick pivots to capitalize on market opportunities, enhancing your ability to align investments with changing goals and circumstances. Proactively anticipating changes empowers you to make informed decisions.

Consider an entrepreneur who invested a portion of their income in tech startups, achieving substantial returns while diversifying their portfolio. Similarly, a consultant who invested in rental real estate created an additional income stream, ensuring financial stability during lean periods.

Viewing income variability as an asset unlocks a world of possibilities. It requires a willingness to learn and take calculated risks, but with flexibility as your ally, you can build a prosperous financial future through thoughtful investments and sustainable growth.

8.4 Trusts and Estate Planning Tools for Legacy Building

Building a financial legacy is about more than just accumulating wealth—it's about ensuring that your assets are managed and distributed according to your wishes. Trusts and other estate planning tools are essential components of this process, offering flexibility, control, and peace of mind for you and your loved ones.

Understanding Trusts and Estate Planning Tools

- **Trusts:** A trust is a legal arrangement that allows a third party (the trustee) to manage assets on behalf of beneficiaries. Trusts can help minimize estate taxes, avoid probate, and provide specific instructions on how assets are to be used or distributed. Common types include:
    - **Revocable Living Trusts:** These allow you to maintain control over your assets during your lifetime and can be adjusted as needed. Upon your passing, the trust assets are distributed without going through probate.
    - **Irrevocable Trusts:** These offer greater tax benefits by transferring ownership of assets

out of your estate but cannot be modified after they are established.

- ○ **Special Needs Trusts:** These ensure that individuals with disabilities receive financial support without jeopardizing their eligibility for government benefits.
- ○ **Charitable Trusts:** These allow you to donate assets to a cause while potentially receiving tax benefits.

- **Wills:** A will is a legal document that outlines how you want your assets distributed after your death. Unlike a trust, a will must go through probate, a court-supervised process that can be time-consuming and public.
- **Power of Attorney:** This legal document grants someone the authority to manage your financial or medical affairs if you become incapacitated.
- **Healthcare Directives:** These specify your medical preferences in case you cannot communicate them yourself, ensuring that decisions align with your values.

Why Estate Planning Matters

Proper estate planning protects your loved ones from unnecessary stress and legal complications. It ensures that your financial legacy is preserved and distributed according to your wishes. Without a plan, your assets may be subject to state laws that determine their distribution, which may not align with your intentions.

Resources for Estate Planning

For individuals interested in creating a will or trust, the following resources can provide valuable guidance and support:

1. **Online Tools:**
   - **Nolo.com:** Offers affordable, easy-to-use templates for wills, trusts, and other estate planning documents. It also provides educational articles on various estate planning topics.
   - **LegalZoom:** An online service that guides users through the process of drafting legal documents, including wills and trusts.

2. **Local Estate Planners:**
   - Consulting a local estate planning attorney ensures personalized advice tailored to your state's laws and your unique financial situation. Many attorneys offer free initial consultations to discuss your needs.
   - Contact your state bar association for a list of licensed estate planning attorneys in your area.

3. **Community Workshops:**
   - Libraries, community centers, and local nonprofit organizations often host free estate planning workshops where you can learn the basics and connect with professionals.

4. **Government Resources:**
   - Check the **Consumer Financial Protection Bureau (CFPB)** or your state's

probate court website for free guides and information on estate planning and probate processes.

Consider a couple, Alex and Jordan, who want to ensure their children's financial future while minimizing legal hurdles. They establish a revocable living trust to hold their home and investments, enabling a seamless transfer of assets to their children upon their passing. Additionally, they draft a will to specify guardianship for their children and designate powers of attorney to manage their financial and medical affairs in case of incapacity. Working with a local estate planning attorney ensures that their plan is comprehensive and compliant with state laws.

Through proactive estate planning, Alex and Jordan achieve peace of mind, knowing that their legacy is protected and their loved ones are provided for. This thoughtful preparation exemplifies the benefits of trusts and other tools in creating a meaningful financial legacy.

8.5 Building a Legacy: Long-Term Wealth and Security

Building wealth is not just about personal gain; it's about laying the groundwork for future generations and making a lasting impact. Legacy planning allows you to create financial security for your heirs, ensuring they have the resources and opportunities to thrive. It's about passing down more than just money—it's about instilling values, offering guidance, and providing a springboard for their success. A well-thought-out legacy plan includes contributing to community and charitable causes, reflecting a commitment to improving the world. This approach secures your family's future and leaves a positive mark on society, creating a ripple effect of generosity and growth.

To establish a lasting financial legacy, a structured approach is vital. Start by setting up trusts and wills as part of your estate planning. Trusts offer a way to manage and distribute your assets, providing control over how and when your wealth is transferred. They can minimize taxes and ensure your assets reach the intended beneficiaries without legal entanglements. Wills, on the other hand, are essential for outlining your wishes and ensuring they are honored after you're gone. Investing in long-term assets like property and businesses can also play a crucial role. These investments often appreciate over time, offering a steady stream of income and building enduring wealth that can be passed down. By carefully selecting and managing these assets, you create a stable financial foundation that supports your legacy goals.

Education and mentorship are key components of legacy building. Passing on financial knowledge and values to the next generation empowers them to make informed decisions and continue the legacy you've started. Teaching children about personal finance from an early age fosters financial literacy and responsibility. It equips them with the tools they need to navigate life's financial challenges with confidence and competence. Mentoring young entrepreneurs in your family or community can also be incredibly rewarding. By sharing your experiences and insights, you help them avoid common pitfalls and encourage innovation and growth. This mentorship extends your influence beyond your immediate family, contributing to a broader culture of success and responsibility.

Consider the story of a philanthropist who dedicated a portion of their wealth to funding educational scholarships. By supporting the education of young minds, they created opportunities for future leaders to rise, ensuring their legacy continued through the achievements of others. This act of giving provided direct benefits to the recipients and inspired others to contribute to similar causes, amplifying the impact. Similarly, a family business owner might focus on planning generational wealth by involving their children in the business early on. By teaching them the ropes and instilling a sense of ownership, they ensure the business thrives across generations. This approach preserves the family's financial stability and reinforces the values of hard work and entrepreneurship.

Building a legacy is about looking beyond immediate needs and focusing on the long-term impact of your financial decisions. It requires thoughtful planning, strategic investments, and a commitment to education and mentorship. By taking these steps, you create a legacy that reflects your values, supports your heirs, and contributes to the greater good. This chapter has explored the importance of long-term financial planning and the role of legacy building in securing future wealth. As you consider your legacy, remember that wealth is not just a measure of financial success but a tool for creating lasting change and empowering future generations.

Conclusion

Remember the vision we set out with: a future where financial instability no longer holds you back. Instead of merely surviving, you are equipped to thrive, using the flexibility of your income to achieve personal and financial goals. The world we envisioned is one where financial resilience is not just a distant dream but a tangible reality.

Beyond the practical steps, mindset plays a pivotal role in your financial journey. Shifting your perspective from fear to confidence, from scarcity to abundance, can be transformative. Embrace this mindset to see setbacks as opportunities for growth and learning. With resilience and adaptability, you can navigate any financial landscape with ease.

Now, it's time to take action. Apply the strategies we've discussed and watch as your financial situation evolves. Start small, but be consistent. Whether it's setting up a budget, opening a savings account, or investing in your future, every step counts. Your journey is unique, and each action you take is a step toward the financial freedom you deserve.

Remember the power of community. Engage with others who share your goals and challenges. Join groups, participate in discussions, and learn from those who have walked a similar path. By building a supportive network, you create a space for shared wisdom and encouragement. Together, you'll find strength in numbers, propelling each other toward success.

I want you to know that you're not alone on this journey. Continued support is available to you, whether through online forums, financial advisors, or community workshops. Seek out the resources that resonate with you and lean on them as you navigate your financial landscape. My experience as an entrepreneur and financial strategist has shown me the importance of having a support system, and I encourage you to build yours.

Financial empowerment is within your reach. With determination, action, and the support of a community, you can transform your financial life. Embrace the journey ahead, knowing that each decision brings you closer to the life you envision. May your path be filled with growth, stability, and the confidence to pursue your dreams.

Empowerment through action and community is the key takeaway from this book. You've gained the tools and insights to take control of your financial future. Now, it's up to you to harness them and create a life of abundance and security. As you move forward, remember that the journey is just as important as the destination. Celebrate each milestone and continue to learn and grow. Your financial freedom is not just a goal; it's a journey filled with possibilities and promise.

References

- *Year-Round Financial Planning Tips For Freelancers*
  https://www.forbes.com/sites/ginnyhogan/2023/04/13/year-round-financial-planning-for-freelancers/

- *Financial knowledge and decision-making skills*
  https://www.consumerfinance.gov/consumer-tools/educator-tools/youth-financial-education/learn/financial-knowledge-decision-making-skills/#:~:text=Strong%20financial%20knowledge%20and%20decision,or%20other%20long%2Dterm%20savings.

- *The impact of income on mental health*
  https://www.thelancet.com/journals/lanpub/article/PIIS2468-2667(22)00094-9/fulltext

- *Self-employed individuals tax center*
  https://www.irs.gov/businesses/small-businesses-self-employed/self-employed-individuals-tax-center

- *Zero-Based Budgeting: Spend Every Penny but Meet Your ...*
  https://www.nerdwallet.com/article/finance/zero-based-budgeting-explained

- *How to Budget With an Irregular Income* https://eringobler.com/budget-with-irregular-income/
- *5 Cash Flow Tips for Seasonal Businesses* https://www.southbaycu.com/impact/blog/2024/5-cash-flow-tips-for-seasonal-businesses/
- *Budgeting Examples: The Success Stories and Case ...* https://fastercapital.com/content/Budgeting-Examples--The-Success-Stories-and-Case-Studies-of-Business-Budgeting.html
- *Debt Avalanche vs. Debt Snowball: What's the Difference?* https://www.investopedia.com/articles/personal-finance/080716/debt-avalanche-vs-debt-snowball-which-best-you.asp
- *The emotional impact of debt: Strategies for effective coping* https://www.cambridgeindependent.co.uk/business/the-emotional-impact-of-debt-strategies-for-effective-copin-9363992/
- *The Best Debt Payoff Apps of 2022* https://www.experian.com/blogs/ask-experian/best-apps-for-paying-off-debt/
- *Freelancer Debt Management: Proven Strategies for ...* https://www.runpollen.com/articles/freelancer-debt-management--proven-strategies-for-paying-down-loans
- *Why Establishing An Emergency Fund Is Essential For ...* https://www.outlookmoney.com/plan/why-

establishing-an-emergency-fund-is-essential-for-freelancers-with-irregular-income

- *How to Save With Irregular Income* https://www.experian.com/blogs/ask-experian/how-to-save-with-irregular-income/
- *8 Ways To Use Financial Mindfulness To Enhance Your Life* https://www.forbes.com/sites/financialfinesse/2024/05/07/financial-mindfulness-the-key-to-enhancing-your-financial-life/
- *Fifteen Smart Strategies to Grow Your Emergency Fund ...* https://www.extracobanks.com/resources/blog/fifteen-smart-strategies-grow-your-emergency-fund-faster
- *How to Set SMART Financial Goals (With Examples)* https://finmasters.com/smart-financial-goals/
- *How to Start Investing in Stocks in 2024 and Beyond* https://www.investopedia.com/articles/basics/06/invest1000.asp
- *How to Make Serious Money: Digital Real Estate for ...* https://leaders.com/articles/investing/digital-real-estate/
- *Solo 401(k) vs. SEP IRA: A Comprehensive Guide for ...* https://www.forusall.com/401k-blog/solo-401-k-vs-sep-ira-a-comprehensive-guide-for-freelancers-and-entrepreneurs

- *How Financial Literacy Affects Household Wealth ...* https://pmc.ncbi.nlm.nih.gov/articles/PMC3554245/
- *The 17 Best Personal Finance Books for Newbies* https://thecfoclub.com/financial-planning-analysis/finance-books-beginners/
- *Unlock the Door to Wealth: 7 Mindset Shifts to Achieve ...* https://www.richdad.com/mindset-shifts-achieve-financial-success
- *5 Tips From A Financial Therapist For Managing ...* https://www.forbes.com/sites/rahkimsabree/2024/08/28/5-tips-from-a-financial-therapist-for-managing-financial-anxiety/
- *Long-and short-term financial planning for life's major events* https://www.citizensbank.com/learning/planning-for-life-events.aspx
- *Make the Leap: 8 Steps for Transitioning to Self-Employment* https://www.thepennyhoarder.com/make-money/transitioning-to-self-employment/
- *The Financial Impacts of Divorce - Coldstream* https://www.coldstream.com/insights/the-financial-impacts-of-divorce/
- *Financial resilience in a new economic regime* https://www.blackrock.com/corporate/about-us/investment-stewardship/insights/financial-resilience-in-new-economic-regime

- *SMART goals (article) | Financial goals*
  https://www.khanacademy.org/college-careers-more/financial-literacy/xa6995ea67a8e9fdd:financial-goals/xa6995ea67a8e9fdd:smart-goals/a/smart-goals

- *How to Manage Lifestyle Inflation*
  https://www.investopedia.com/articles/personal-finance/092313/how-manage-lifestyle-inflation.asp

- *The Best Personal Finance and Budgeting Apps for 2024* https://www.pcmag.com/picks/the-best-personal-finance-services

- *Guide to Legacy Planning*
  https://www.northwesternmutual.com/life-and-money/guide-to-legacy-planning/

About the Author

Alex Bradley is an experienced entrepreneur and financial strategist with a unique perspective on side hustles and small business management. Growing up on a farm, she witnessed her parents' struggles with unpredictable income, which motivated her to earn advanced business degrees and gain corporate experience.

As a real estate investor, Alex has successfully managed multiple income streams, demonstrating that financial stability is achievable. Her practical knowledge in budgeting and cash flow management enables her to inspire those facing irregular income challenges.

A strong advocate for financial literacy, Alex serves on nonprofit boards and volunteers to empower others with the tools they need to achieve financial freedom. When she's not consulting or writing, she enjoys spending time with her family, gardening, and traveling.

www.ingramcontent.com/pod-product-compliance
Lightning Source LLC
Chambersburg PA
CBHW031421210526
45464CB00005B/1984